Cruisers

Antony Preston

Prentice Hall

Englewood Cliffs N.J.

A Bison Book

First US edition published by
Prentice-Hall, Inc.
Englewood Cliffs
New Jersey 07632

Copyright © 1980 by Bison Books
Limited

Produced by
Bison Books Limited
4 Cromwell Place
London SW7

Library of Congress Catalog
Card Number: 79-89592

ISBN 013-194902-0

Printed in Hong Kong

pp 2–3: *The old armoured cruisers, HMS
Suffolk (left)* and USS *Brooklyn (right),
at Vladivostock during the Allied
Intervention, January 1919.*

Below: USS *Salt Lake City (CA-25)
and* Pensacola *at Pearl Harbor on
31 October 1943.*

Contents

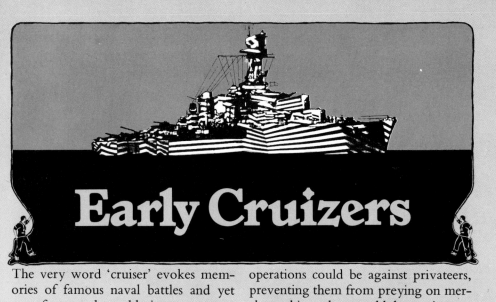

Early Cruizers

The very word 'cruiser' evokes memories of famous naval battles and yet very few people could give an accurate description of a cruiser's function as a warship. In fact even naval historians have difficulty in defining just what a cruiser does. The answer would depend on the period chosen, since cruisers have been constantly changing in the last hundred years. In many ways it is easier to say what a cruiser is *not*, for she is neither battleship nor destroyer, and yet she has often fought decisive actions against both types.

The word 'cruizing' was used in the eighteenth and early nineteenth century to describe independent operations by a single ship, unattached to any squadron. 'Cruizers', therefore, were usually frigates but equally were often smaller sloops and brigs, and very rarely ships-of-the-line. The essential meaning of the word was a description of function, not a classification of a ship-type. These operations could be against privateers, preventing them from preying on merchant ships; they could be against an enemy's shipping, or they could be merely to provide a distant squadron with intelligence.

The term continued to be used when steam was introduced, but in the 1880s it came to be applied increasingly to a broad category of warships, smaller than the battleship and the big steam frigate, and known as steam sloops and corvettes. As their function was to operate independently they were correctly described as cruisers, but because they were quite sizeable warships, and ranked above the traditional steam sloop in importance, they came to be thought of as a separate category. By 1889 the last of the Royal Navy's big steam frigates, HMS *Raleigh*, was rerated as a cruiser on the Navy List and a new category of warship was created. Where the Royal Navy led others followed and within a

very short time the assortment of sloops, corvettes and frigates in all navies had become cruisers.

As a cruiser's main task was to catch commerce-raiding warships and to prey on enemy shipping, speed was an important attribute. The engines of the day were cumbersome, with reciprocating pistons, and as they were coal-eaters it was necessary to carry masts and yards as well, to save coal on long passages. This in turn limited the amount of armour which could be applied to protect the hull of a cruiser. In the 1870s and early 1880s the British and Russians tried their hands at producing 'belted' cruisers, but the weight of wrought-iron armour was so great that the narrow armoured belt was submerged when the ships were at their load draught. Thereafter designers restricted themselves to providing an arched steel deck, which protected the machinery and magazines from shellfire.

As early as 1871 the British industrialist, Sir William Armstrong, proposed to a Committee on Designs for Ships of War that the growing efficiency of guns and shells would defeat side armour. Since armour could not produce invulnerability, he pointed out, it might as well be abandoned. Instead the weight could be devoted to armouring the bows of a warship, while a number of watertight compartments below the waterline could limit flooding from hits elsewhere. This extreme viewpoint was not accepted by the two admirals on the committee and they recommended a thick armoured deck as well as the compartmentation suggested by Armstrong. In 1879 Armstrong's shipyard at Low Walker on the Tyne received an order for a gunboat from Chile, followed three months later by another for two sisters from China. In this trio Armstrong's ideas were developed; two heavy guns and a partial deck over the machinery, boilers and magazines below the waterline, were introduced.

These three ships were hardly big enough to act as cruisers but they provided valuable experience for Armstrong's chief designer, George Rendel, when he designed a cruiser for Chile in 1880-81. She was the *Esmeralda*, a ship which, according to the Royal Navy's Chief Surveyor, Nathaniel Barnaby, not only made the fortune of Armstrong's company, but also led to an increase in the speeds of all warships and caused sails to be abandoned. The *Esmeralda* and her Royal Navy contemporary HMS *Mersey*, had a complete deck instead of the earlier partial deck, a vast improvement over previous ideas, and as the Chilean ship also carried two single 10-inch guns she created a tremendous impression of fighting power on a relatively modest displacement.

Time was to show that the *Esmeralda* was a poor seaboat, with freeboard sacrificed in favour of gunpower. The continuous armoured deck was not

The frigate USS Kearsage *exemplifies the original 'cruiser'. In 1864 she sank the Confederate raider* Alabama *off Cherbourg. She remained in service until wrecked in 1894.*

Below: *The French armoured cruiser*
Pothuau *was developed from the Dupuy
de Lôme. The 'plough' bow, the high
freeboard and the small turrets became
familiar French trademarks, but they were
not good sea boats.*

Above: *The Wampanoag and her
sisters were a bold attempt to create fast
commerce-raiding cruisers but fell short of
expectations. In 1869 all five were
renamed, Wampanoag becoming the
USS Florida. She is seen here dry docked
at Brooklyn Navy Yard in 1874.*

Above: *The Italian armoured cruiser*
Vettor Pisani, *built in 1892-99,*
followed British practice but had much
lighter armament than her contemporaries.
Despite this she served through World
War I.

three inches thick throughout its length and the normal coal stowage did not approach the 600 tons claimed. She did, however, give an impression of great fighting power, and for overseas navies prestige and reputation counted for at least as much as actual capabilities. The Italians bought a slightly larger version, the *Giovanni Bausan*, and soon everybody wanted to buy 'Elswick' cruisers, so-called because building was soon moved up-river to Elswick-on-Tyne. Japan bought two; Greece ordered one; China two and Italy one; all within five years. The biggest advantage of the Elswick cruisers, apart from their apparent superiority over all their contemporaries, was the fact that they could be built quickly and cheaply, because they were more lightly built than contemporary Royal Navy cruisers. British shipyards were at the height of their Golden Age, with a reputation for quality, speed of delivery and cheapness, and Armstrong's could provide guns from its own foundries, keeping costs even more firmly under control. Although not sufficiently seaworthy or robust to meet British requirements, they suited the smaller navies very well.

The French broke away from the 'protective deck' concept in 1888, when they designed the *Dupuy de Lôme*. Using the new Harvey steel, the designer Emile Bertin was able to armour the whole length of waterline with a narrow belt. A protective deck was also provided at the lower edge of the belt, to stop shells which plunged over the top of the belt, and below it was another partial thin deck to catch any splinters penetrating the main deck. Coal stowed between these decks in a 'cellular layer' or *tranche cellulaire* provided further protection against shells, while the watertight compartments were filled with cellulose, which was meant to swell and

11

fill any holes in the outside plating made by shell-hits. The *Dupuy de Lôme* caused a great sensation when she appeared in 1893 (she took five years to build, as against three for the *Esmeralda*), and inspired the French Navy to build a new series of fast commerce-raiding cruisers based on her design. Like the *Esmeralda*, she had drawbacks which only came to light after she had been in service for some years; the narrow waterline belt was usually submerged at full load, and in practice the compartments were almost impossible to keep fully watertight. Another disadvantage of the cellular layer was that it made for very awkward stowage of coal; the ship would not steam for any great length of time before it became impossible to keep up the supply of coal from the most distant bunkers.

The next step was to concentrate the armour over more important areas, in exactly the same manner as battleship designers had been forced to, because of the impossibility of providing plating all over. The result was that a new type of cruiser appeared: the 'armoured' as opposed to the 'protected' cruiser, with a belt of medium-thickness armour and larger guns. They were in effect second-class battleships and it was realised that they were faster than, as well protected and nearly as well armed as many of the smaller battleships. They were also in many cases bigger than contemporary battleships because enormous boiler-power was needed to drive them at high speed. Predictably it was Armstrong's yard which seized the opportunity. Chile had sold the *Esmeralda* to Japan in 1894 and so the following year Elswick started work on Job No 639, a new *Esmeralda*. Unlike previous Elswick cruisers she had a narrow waterline belt of 6-inch armour in addition to her protective deck and carried single 8-inch quick-firing guns on the forecastle and stern. She was hailed as the most powerful warship in the world, and in the passion for statistics which prevailed in Victorian England, it was claimed that her two 8-inch and sixteen 6-inch guns delivered a greater weight of shells per minute than the most powerful battleship afloat. As always, the extremist view was that battleships could easily be replaced by numerous *Esmeraldas*.

The truth was that, like her earlier namesake, she suffered from carrying too much weight at either end and the forward gun could not be fired in moderately rough weather. The ship

Below: *The French d'Entrecasteaux, built at Toulon in 1894–99, relied on a protective deck of 2.2-inch steel and steamed at 19 knots. In common with other cruisers intended to serve on the trade routes she was sheathed with wood and copper to reduce fouling of the bottom plating.*

was considerably overweight, and so only 2 feet of the 7-foot deep armour belt remained over the waterline when she was fully laden. Like the earlier Elswick cruisers she was very lightly built and not capable of hard driving in all weathers, the paramount requirement of a cruiser. Time was to show, too, that having the guns in open-backed shields would expose their crews to a deadly hail of splinters in battle. The *Esmeralda* was lucky not to have her weaknesses exposed in action and she finally went to the scrapyard in 1929 after an honourable but uneventful career.

The *Esmeralda* was closer to the French idea of a commerce-raiding cruiser, but the next Elswick cruisers were definitely in a more powerful category. The Chileans, with an eye to quarrels with their neighbours, ordered the *O'Higgins* in 1896 before the *Esmeralda* had started her trials. She was given four single 8-inch guns in turrets forward and aft and a heavy secondary battery of 6-inch and 4.7-inch guns. Her vitals were protected by a belt which varied from 5 inches to 7 inches in thickness. She was also a much more imposing ship than the *Esmeralda*, with three tall funnels and her 6-inch guns in armoured casemates along the side at main deck level. These were individual armoured boxes, designed to protect the guns from that destructive hail of splinters which could be inflicted by a ship armed with the latest quick-firing guns.

The *O'Higgins* proved to be what Armstrong's customers wanted and Japan ordered the *Asama* and *Tokiwa* shortly afterwards, followed by the similar *Idzumo* and *Iwate* in 1898. This quartet of cruisers was to form the backbone of the Imperial Japanese Fleet during the war against Russia and its outstanding performance did much to foster an inflated idea of the armoured cruiser's worth.

When war broke out (undeclared, as it was to be 37 years later) the *Asama* went into action on the first day, 9 February 1904. Under the command of Admiral Uriu, she and the rest of the 4th Division attacked the Russian cruiser *Varyag* without warning while she lay in the Korean harbour of Chemulpo. The *Varyag* sank at her moorings, having failed to inflict any casualties on the Japanese ships. The *Asama* was again in action in the indecisive Battle of the Yellow Sea in August, and the *Idzumo*, *Iwate* and *Tokiwa* brought the Russian

Below: *The Japanese armoured cruiser* Iwate *was built at Elswick in 1898-1901, and steamed at 20 knots. She and her sister* Idzumo *formed part of the battle line at Tsushima, giving rise to the illusion that battlecruisers could serve as fast battleships. She survived the two world wars as a training ship and was scrapped in 1947.*

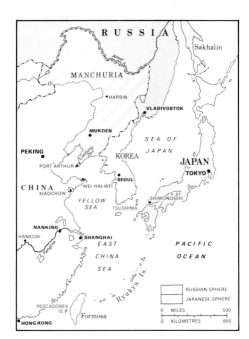

Above: *The Far East in 1904, with Russia facing Japan.*

cruiser *Rurik* to bay in the Battle of Ulsan on 4 August. The *Rurik* was sunk and the armoured cruisers *Gromoboi* and *Rossia* sustained heavy damage. The *Idzumo* and *Tokiwa* got off lightly but the *Iwate* had many casualties from a fire caused by a Russian 8-inch shell bursting in a casemate.

All four armoured cruisers were in the 2nd Division at the Battle of Tsushima on 27 May 1905, with *Idzumo* flying the flag of Vice-Admiral Kamimura and *Iwate* flying the flag of Rear-Admiral Shimamura. They went into action astern of Admiral Togo's battleships, six armoured cruisers in all, including the French-built *Adzuma* and the German-built *Yakumo*. Another two armoured cruisers served with Togo's four battleships in the 1st Division, the Italian-built *Kasuga* and *Nisshin*, under the command of Vice-Admiral Misu.

The flagship *Mikasa* opened fire on the *Kniaz Suvorov* at a distance of 7000 yards and 10 minutes later the cruisers were all firing at the Russian battle line. The Russians fired well in the opening stages of the action; the *Kasuga* was hit by a 12-inch shell and her sister *Nisshin* had an 8-inch gun cut in half by a shell. At 1428 the *Asama* was hit aft by a 12-inch shell which put her steering gear out of action and by the time her damage-control parties had repaired the damage the rest of her squadron had vanished into the mist.

The Russians' fate was sealed, with their line thrown into confusion by the heavy Japanese fire. For over two hours

they tried to push their way past the Japanese, but without success, as Admiral Togo counter-marched each time to frustrate the plan. The *Asama* caught up with the Battle Fleet after 1500, just in time to join in a cannonade against the Russian ships. Apart from a 12-inch hit on the *Nisshin*, Kamimura's division received light hits which caused no serious damage. At 1555 the main Russian force was sighted; in the gun duel which followed the *Nisshin* was hit on her conning tower, and splinters penetrated the vision-slits and wounded Admiral Misu. The *Asama* was out of luck too, for a 6-inch shell went through her after funnel, and the loss of draught in the boiler-room slowed her down again.

The confused visibility suited the cruisers, for they were able to engage enemy battleships at a range which favoured their own medium-calibre guns, which fired faster than the battleships' 10-inch and 12-inch guns. The action degenerated into a *mêlée*, with the Russians losing all formation, although individual ships continued to fight with desperate bravery. When the survivors tried to escape it was the turn of the Japanese torpedo boats and destroyers to pick them off with torpedoes. Out of five modern protected cruisers with the Baltic Fleet only three survived. The *Oleg, Aurora* and *Jemtchug* reached the Philippines and were interned at Manila, but the *Svietlana* was sunk by the Japanese small cruisers *Otawa* and *Niitaka* and the *Izumrud* was wrecked North of Vladivostok.

The heroic work done by the eight modern armoured cruisers at Tsushima might have guaranteed the type a long

Right: *Togo's fleet crosses the Russians' 'T'.*

Below: *The Russian Baltic Fleet's long voyage to disaster.*

lease of life, but already events were in train which would reduce them to obsolescence within three years. In 1904 Admiral Sir John Fisher became the Royal Navy's First Sea Lord and immediately set up a Committee on Designs to give effect to his ideas for new ships. The most revolutionary was his battleship *Dreadnought*, which had more than double the armament of previous battleships and three knots more speed. The secret of *Dreadnought*'s high speed of 21 knots was the adoption of the relatively untried Parsons turbine, and Fisher decided to produce a *Dreadnought*-equivalent of the armoured cruiser, to fulfill the same role as the older type. But instead of 8-inch, 9.2-inch or 10-inch guns, this new armoured cruiser was to have 12-inch guns, to enable her to fight off battleships on more equal terms. Naturally the jump from 21 to 25 knots could not be achieved on the same displacement as *Dreadnought* without some sacrifice, and in this case one twin 12-inch gun mounting had to go and armour was restricted to the same 6-inch armour belt as the existing cruisers. When questioned about the wisdom of pitting such ships against well-protected battleships Fisher was apt to dismiss the problem by claiming that the ships' speed would enable them to 'keep out of trouble'.

The new ships certainly fulfilled their designers' requirements when they made 25.5 knots on trials. Their appearance virtually killed off the old armoured cruiser and for a while there was even talk of the smaller cruiser disappearing. The principal roles envisaged for them were to scout ahead of the battle fleet, to

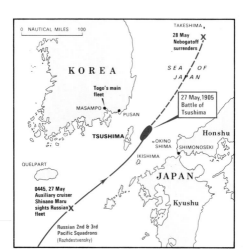

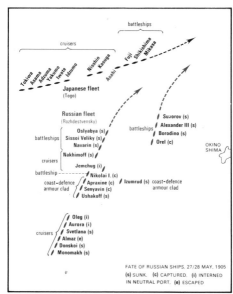

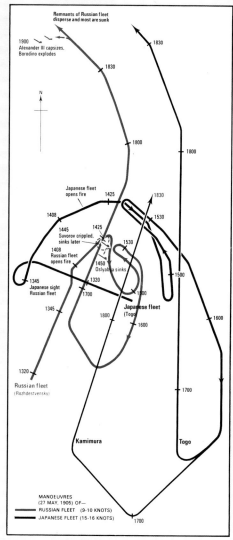

Above: *The Russian protected cruiser* Varyag *was built in the United States in 1898–1900, and was sunk at Chemulpo in Korea at the outbreak of the Russo-Japanese War. After salvage and a decade of service as the Japanese* Soya *she was returned in 1916 to Russian ownership.*

Below: *The* Geier *was one of a series of small German cruisers built in 1888–95 for colonial service. Note the barquentine rig for economising on coal during long passages and the bowsprit. She was interned by the United States in 1914.*

Above: *The main fleet engagement at Tsushima.*

run down and destroy enemy armoured cruisers on the trade routes and to finish off crippled battleships in the closing stages of a fleet action. The value of 12-inch guns in the last two roles was open to question, as it was a very expensive solution to the problem, but for the scouting role it was claimed that 12-inch guns would enable these ships to push a reconnaissance past a screen of cruisers, and would enable them to close within gun-range of the enemy battle line (something a cruiser would not normally dare to do).

The term 'dreadnought armoured cruiser' was too cumbersome to last long and in 1913 the term 'battlecruiser' was coined for the *Invincible* Class and its successors, the *Indefatigable* and *Lion* Classes. It was, with hindsight, an unfortunate choice, for it suggested a ship of capital rank, whereas a look at the design of *Invincible* reveals that she was no more than a turbine-driven cruiser,

armed with four twin 12-inch gun turrets instead of the previous mixed armament of 9.2-inch and 7.5-inch guns. What nobody could foresee was that no admiral would be able to resist the temptation of strengthening his battle line with ships carrying eight 12-inch guns – in other words, they would be mistaken for fast battleships, which they most definitely could not be. As we shall see, this confusion of title and function was to have tragic consequences.

The glamour of the *Dreadnought* and the *Invincible* Class focused attention on major warships but the traditional cruiser was still very much in being. Admittedly Fisher had no time for the small cruiser, which he despised as being 'too weak to fight and too slow to run away'. The protected cruiser had been divided into three types: 1st, 2nd and 3rd Class, ranging from enormous ships on a par with armoured cruisers down to ships

Below: *The old British–built ironclad* Deutschland *was rebuilt as a grosskreuzer in 1894–97 and then served abroad. She is seen here at Port Arthur in 1898, with a French protected cruiser in the background, either the* Tage *or* Amiral Cécille.

Above: *The design of this French armoured cruiser was changed so many times that she finally emerged in 1909 as a separate type. The Ernest Renan reached 24 knots on trials but belonged to a dying breed. She survived until 1931 as a training ship.*

Right: *The Russian armoured cruiser Bayan in 1903. She was captured by the Japanese in 1904 and renamed the Aso.*

Above: *SMS Kolberg was built in 1908-10 as the first of a class of four light cruisers armed with twelve 4.1-inch guns and capable of 25.5 knots. She ended her days as the French Colmar, having been handed over as war booty in 1920.*

Below: *HMS Sentinel, built in 1903-05, was one of a series of scout cruisers with only light armament, for leading destroyer flotillas. She is seen here on trials, minus her 12-pounder (3-inch) guns. But in 1911-12 she was re-armed with 4-inch guns.*

little better than gunboats. The term 'scout' came into vogue at the turn of the century for the latest 3rd Class cruisers and for a while the Royal Navy built no other cruisers.

The scout broke away from previous cruiser policy in being designed to work with destroyers rather than with big ships. In fact their speed of 25 knots was geared to the sea speed of contemporary destroyers, and this in turn dictated that they had destroyer-type machinery and only token protection. The armament was restricted to 3-inch or 4-inch guns, as in destroyers, and a couple of torpedo tubes, but they were big enough to accommodate the senior officer of the flotilla and his staff, and could easily keep up with the more frail destroyers. What they could not do, however, was operate on the trade routes or reconnoitre efficiently for the fleet.

Other navies, particularly the French, Italian and American showed a declining interest in smaller cruisers, preferring to build very big armoured cruisers. The knowledge that Germany was continuing to build small cruisers was sufficient warning to the British that they must get back into the game. In 1908 work began on a new design, in defiance of Fisher's known dislike of cruisers, and the first of the class was ready at the end of 1910. The five *Bristol* Class were a great improvement over the scouts, being bigger and sturdier ships. With experience gained from the scout *Amethyst*, the *Bristol* Class ships were driven by steam turbines at 25 knots. This equalled the speed of the scouts. The extra 1000 tons of weight were used to provide an armoured deck and two 6-inch guns, in addition to ten 4-inch guns.

The *Bristol* Class makes an interesting contrast with its contemporary German *Kolberg* Class (see table below).

On paper the German cruiser was superior, particularly as she had a small patch of splinter-proof side armour over her machinery and boilers and had a two-knot advantage in speed. The maximum speed of 27 knots, however, was achieved by overload and in practice they were only good for 25 knots at 20,000 horsepower. Although it was widely believed that the 4.1-inch gun could outrange the 6-inch gun (on the basis of comparisons with the very elderly British 6-inch designed 15 years before), and that the lighter shell allowed a higher rate of fire, time was to show this was fallacious. In practice the heavier British gun could not only outrange the 4.1-inch and inflict more damage, but could also shoot more accurately at extreme range because its ballistics were superior.

Both sides continued to build their 'Town' Class cruisers, but the Germans clung to the idea of a large number of light guns while the British moved on to a much heavier armament. The next class after the *Bristol*, the *Weymouth* Class, were very similar but dropped the 4-inch guns and had a uniform armament of eight 6-inch. They also had a longer forecastle, because seaworthiness, in British designs, was of prime importance. In the next design, the *Chatham* Class of 1911–12, the forecastle was extended two-thirds of the length of the ship, allowing five of the eight 6-inch guns to be mounted at maximum height. In this class the British finally achieved the sort of cruiser they wanted, with sufficient endurance to hunt down commerce-raiders across the oceans yet with sufficient speed and gun-armament to serve as fleet scouts. With their seaworthiness and heavy gunpower they were to prove tough opponents in battle, and their elegant silhouette, with four slim funnels and a distinctive 'plough' shaped bow, set a new standard. A follow-on class, the *Birminghams*, differed only in having an extra 6-inch gun on the forecastle, and when the Greeks ordered two cruisers in 1914 they chose the *Birmingham* design without hesitation, despite having ordered a battlecruiser from Germany. Four ships of this type were also ordered by Australia, the *Sydney*, *Melbourne* and *Brisbane* of the *Chatham* type, and the *Adelaide* of the slightly larger *Birmingham* type.

	Bristol	*Kolberg*
Displacement (normal):	4,800 tons	4,350 tons
Length:	430 feet	428 feet
Beam:	47 feet	46 feet
Horsepower:	22,000 shp	30,000 shp (max)
Speed:	25 knots	27 knots
Guns:	2 × 6-inch 10 × 4-inch	12 × 4.1-inch

The United States Navy had not followed a very coherent policy of cruiser-building. The reasons were partly historical and partly financial. Going back as far as the War of Independence, the War of 1812 and the Civil War, individual warships had achieved great fame as commerce-raiders, and there was a natural tendency to think in terms of fast cruisers for this single purpose, much like the French. There was also the problem of the severe financial stringency under which the US Navy laboured during the 1870s and 1880s. Even when the threat of war with Spain caused money to be spent on the Navy, it tended to be spent on capital ships first, monitors and then cruisers. Unlike the British, the Americans had no vast seaborne trade to protect and so there was no compulsion to build anything like the standard 2nd Class cruisers which British shipyards turned out in large numbers in the 1890s.

When the Americans did build cruisers they built them big. The *Pennsylvania* Class of 1899-1908 displaced 13,680 tons, were 502ft long and had four 8-inch and 14 6-inch guns. The *Tennessee* Class were nearly 1000 tons bigger and had two twin 10-inch gun-turrets. The last of the classic commerce-raiding cruisers built were the *Columbia* and *Minneapolis* in 1890-94. They were intended to catch transatlantic liners, and so had two 6-inch guns forward as bow-chasers, with an 8-inch gun aft to deal with any pursuing warship. In a well-publicised race in July 1895 the *Columbia* maintained 18 knots for seven

days and beat the Hamburg-Amerika liner *August-Viktoria*. However they had their drawbacks and they were so expensive to run that they were both laid up, only to be hurriedly recommissioned for the war with Spain in 1898.

The French, having convinced themselves that the whole *raison d'être* of a navy was to operate against commerce rather than fight an enemy fleet, stopped building small cruisers in the mid-1890s. Developments of the *Dupuy de Lôme* were built in considerable numbers, but in spite of their imposing appearance they were not good steamers and not particularly well protected, when compared with the British ships they were intended to fight. All fast cruisers needed a large number of boilers to provide the power for their machinery, and this meant three or four tall funnels to provide the necessary draught, but the French set a new standard in the *Jeanne d'Arc* in 1903, with *six* funnels. The dire influence of the Minister of Marine, Camille Pelletan, in the early 1900s meant that France all but dropped out of the cruiser-business. When the decision was reversed, and 10 scout cruisers were ordered, it was 1914 and the plans had to be shelved.

The Japanese were closely associated with the British, and so they tended to follow Royal Navy ideas on design. As their armoured cruisers had behaved so well at Tsushima they decided to go ahead with their plans for building their own armoured cruisers. The plans had been drawn up in 1903-04 to take

maximum advantage of Japanese industrial capacity. It was not possible to build heavy gun-turrets, but armour plates of up to 7 inches in thickness could be machined in Japanese foundries. The war with Russia accelerated the plans, for the Japanese Diet wanted to ensure that the Navy would not be too weakened by war losses to deter any other aggressors. Armoured cruisers could be built faster than battleships, and the early war experience confirmed their usefulness, and so the keel of the first ship, the *Tsukuba* was laid in January 1905. She and her sister *Ikoma* were built at Kure Dockyard, but were not finished for two or three years. They were handsome ships with two well-spaced, tall funnels. They were also the most heavily armed cruisers of their day with 12-inch guns in two twin turrets, a dozen 6-inch and another dozen 4.7-inch. Although not as fast as some foreign armoured cruisers, 20.5 knots gave them a margin of 2.5 knots over contemporary battleships.

Unfortunately for the Japanese and their bold attempt to bridge the gap between the battleship and the cruiser, the building of HMS *Dreadnought* and HMS *Invincible* rendered them obsolete almost as soon as they were commissioned. Ironically the good liaison between the Japanese and the British meant that details of the *Tsukuba* had been made available to the Royal Navy, and she had been one of the reasons for

Top: *The fast commerce raider USS* Columbia *was reliable but heavy on coal.*

Centre: *HMS* Southampton, *one of the new breed of 6-inch gunned cruisers.*

Above: *The Japanese* Kurama *was a hybrid, with the hull of an armoured cruiser and the two twin 12-inch guns of a pre-Dreadnought battleship.*

arming the *Invincible* with 12-inch guns, rather than lighter guns. Another two ships of enlarged type were built, the *Kurama* and *Ibuki*, with four twin 8-inch gun-mountings instead of the single 6-inch. It was typical of the Japanese that they should buy Curtis turbines from the United States for the *Ibuki*, to gain experience with the new machinery and give her a speed of 22.5 knots.

The Russians built only four more armoured cruisers, the three *Admiral Makarov* Class similar to older ships, and a powerful new ship built in England, the *Rurik*. She was one of the most powerful cruisers afloat, with 10-inch and 8-inch guns and a speed of 21 knots. In 1912 a new programme of smaller cruisers was started, with eight *Admiral Butakov* Class laid down in Russian yards and two *Nevelskoi* Class ordered in Germany. The *Nevelskoi* Class had a heavy armament by contemporary standards, eight 5.1-inch (130mm) guns but the bigger *Admiral Butakov* Class went even further, with fifteen 5.1-inch guns. The Russians were trying hard to recover from their humiliating defeat by the Japanese, and spared no expense in rebuilding the Fleet.

The Italians were heavily influenced by the British, and for some years built variants of Elswick designs, but they also made some highly original contributions of their own. Some of their so-called 'torpedo cruisers' would have been rated as torpedo gunboats in the Royal Navy, but they persevered with the idea of high-speed ships armed with torpedo tubes, and produced a series of remarkable *esploratori*, the equivalent of the British scouts. The *Quarto*, built in 1909-13, could make 28 knots in service with four-shaft steam turbines, and had an armament of a dozen light guns as well as two deck torpedo tubes. In addition she could be rapidly converted for mine-laying, with a capacity of 200 mines. Two more *esploratori*, the *Nino Bixio* and *Marsala* were less successful, and could not get within three knots of their designed speed.

The next step was to bring the size down to that of a destroyer, with the 1000-ton *Alessandro Poerio* Class. Laid down in 1913, these three hybrids carried roughly double the armament of conventional destroyers. They and the following *Carlo Mirabello* (1780 tons) were formidable destroyers, but never fulfilled their designers' hopes of functioning as small cruisers. The *Mirabellos* were given a 6-inch gun on the fore-

castle, but this merely accentuated their weak points by making them roll and pitch in heavy weather. By being unable to keep the sea in all weathers they failed the first requirement of a cruiser.

The British, having created the successful 'Town' Class, decided that a new class of smaller cruiser was needed to work with destroyers. Since the building of the first scouts in 1904 the speed of destroyers had risen from 25 to 30 knots, and in 1912 the decision was made to produce a new intermediate type, more powerful than the scouts, five knots faster but carrying two 6-inch guns. The *Chatham* and *Birmingham* Classes had introduced a small strip of armour on the waterline, intended to keep destroyer-sized (3-inch and 4-inch) shells from penetrating boiler-rooms and machinery spaces, rather than to protect them against heavy shells. This feature was to be incorporated into the new small cruisers, but in a much improved form. The basic design was similar to the latest scouts, the *Active* Class, and to have provided a worthwhile amount of side armour would not only have pushed up displacement (and cost) unreasonably,

Above: *The Russians ordered the* Rurik *from Britain. She was in the Baltic in 1915.*

but would also have made the desired speed of 29-30 knots impossible to attain.

Normally armour plates were bolted to the hull, which had to be strengthened to take this additional 'skin', but in the new cruisers it was decided to build the hull with a longitudinal strake of 2-inch high-tensile steel in addition to the normal 1-inch side plating. In effect this made the armouring part of the hull and provided sufficient structural strength to allow the rest of the hull to be lighter. Weight was also saved by using the fast-running turbines and boilers normally used in destroyers, and by providing oil fuel. Previously coal had been used in all cruisers, as it had the additional advantage of providing a measure of protection against hits from shells and torpedoes. Oil has greater thermal efficiency than coal, and the weight of coal saved could be used for higher speed as well as armour. Certainly the new 'light armoured cruisers', better known as the *Arethusa* Class, could not

have been built on such a small displacement without these advances in technology.

At about the same time the British established a precedent by abolishing the cumbersome and irrelevant grading system of cruisers into scouts, 1st, 2nd and 3rd Class, protected and armoured, etc. Instead the armoured cruisers and big deck-protected cruisers were lumped together as 'cruisers', while all the old protected cruisers, the scouts, 'Towns' and the new *Arethusa* Class became 'light cruisers'. Exactly where the dividing line came was not specifically laid down, but there was a general consensus among the world's navies that light cruisers had guns up to 6-inch calibre, whereas the bigger ships had guns of higher calibre. Significantly the hybrid battlecruisers were no longer included in the cruiser category, and everyone had come to accept them as a species of capital ship ranking just below the battleship.

When war broke out in August 1914 the 360-odd cruisers in the world were a collection of ancient and modern. The Royal Navy led the world with 114 of all sizes, followed by the French, German, United States and Japanese navies. Battleships being prestige units, it was inevitable that much of the fighting would be done by smaller units, and this provided the cruiser with its *rationale*. After all the comparisons of gunpower and speed had been made, the cruiser was the largest warship which could be built in reasonable numbers, and she would therefore be called on to perform the widest variety of tasks.

	Arethusa	Birmingham
Displacement:	3,530 tons	5,400 tons
Length:	450 feet	430 feet
Beam:	39 feet	49 feet 9 inches
Horsepower:	30,000 shp	22,000 shp
Speed:	29 knots	24.75 knots
Guns:	2 × 6-inch 6 × 4-inch	9 × 6-inch

Right: *The Dresden, typical of the series of German light cruisers built from 1902 to 1914. Note the elaborate bow scroll, a hangover from the 19th century, and the mast stepped in front of the bridge. It was tacitly assumed by most designers that most fighting would be done on the broadside.*

Below: *HMS Royalist, one of the new 'light armoured cruisers' which followed the Chatham Class in 1912. Intended only for North Sea work in company with destroyers, they were four knots faster. Although cramped and lively in rough weather they proved eminently suitable for expansion in later classes.*

On the High Seas

The opening weeks of the First World War seemed to confirm pre-war notions about how navies would function. There were a number of German cruisers in the Far East and a small Austro-Hungarian squadron. The German ships were the modern armoured cruisers *Scharnhorst* and *Gneisenau* and the light cruisers *Emden*, *Dresden*, *Leipzig* and *Nürnberg* under the command of Vice-Admiral Maximilian von Spee, flying his flag in the *Scharnhorst*.

A month before the outbreak of war von Spee took his East Asian Cruiser Squadron on a cruise in the South Pacific, leaving Fregatten-Kapitän Karl von Müller in the *Emden* as Senior officer at Tsingtao, the German base on the northern coast of China. As soon as the news of impending war was received von Müller brought his ship to a state of readiness, with the result that he was able to put to sea on 31 July 1914 ready to harass enemy shipping in the Far East. Two days later, when a state of war existed between Russia and Germany, the *Emden* captured a Russian merchantman, the SS *Rjäsan*, and sent her back to Tsingtao. In the meantime the base prepared colliers and supply ships to replenish the main squadron in the South Pacific. All depended on the attitude of the Japanese. If they remained

neutral von Spee's cruisers would find easy pickings in the Indian Ocean or could choose their moment to make their way back to Germany around Cape Horn, but if they joined the Allies they would immediately attack Tsingtao and rob von Spee of his base.

Below: *The* Ikoma, *like her sister* Tsukuba, *was an earlier version of the* Ibuki *Class. They were upgraded from armoured cruisers to battlecruisers in 1912. The* Ikoma *was employed in the hunt for von Spee's ships in 1914.*

Above: *SMS* Königsberg *in a setting in East Africa, the backcloth for her exploits: the sinking of HMS* Pegasus *at Zanzibar and her last stand in the Rufiji River. Note how the flaps on the port casement are lowered to allow the 10.5cm gun a clear arc of fire.*

In the event this is what happened and von Spee chose to take his ships to the coast of South America, close to neutral harbours where he could continue to get coal, and well out of the way of the powerful Japanese Navy. However it was decided that it was still worth sending one cruiser into the Indian Ocean to cause disruption. The *Emden* had left the doomed outpost of Tsingtao and had joined her squadron on 12 August. She was ideal for the task, being the fastest in the squadron, and so two days later she left her squadron mates and headed for the Palau Islands accompanied by a collier.

From the Palaus, east of the Philippines, the *Emden* went south to Timor and then headed west for Java, taking care to hide her true destination as far as possible. When she reached the Lombok

Strait von Müller decided that it was time to adopt a disguise, and soon the ship sported a fourth funnel made of wood and canvas. The result was that she reached the Bay of Bengal unrecognised by the British, French and Japanese warships hunting for her just at the time when the initial panic had subsided and shipping was beginning to get back to its pre-war level.

The first capture was made on 10 September, the Greek collier *Pontoporros*. She was pressed into service to serve the *Emden*'s needs. During the following week another five ships were captured, four of them were sunk and the fifth was used to transport the prisoners. Von Müller interpreted the Prize Regulations scrupulously and released the prize with her prisoners before sinking another two British merchantmen. Despite this carnage the Allies did not know the *Emden* was in the area until a neutral Italian merchantman reported that she had been stopped and searched by a German cruiser. The news was sufficient to bring trade to a standstill once more, with navigation lights extinguished and worried shipowners holding cargoes back in port.

The cause of all this havoc was no longer in the area, having slipped away to look for targets off Rangoon before doubling back to Madras. On 22 September she stood about two miles offshore and bombarded the oil storage tanks. Two tanks were set ablaze, three more were damaged and random shots fell in the city and damaged shipping in the harbour. The effect was exactly what von Müller had hoped for, pandemonium in the city, a blow to British prestige and all shipping brought to a halt only a day after it had restarted. The side effects were even worse; the value of exports out of Madras, one of Indian's biggest ports, fell by more than 60 per cent.

. The culprit disappeared from the scene in as mysterious a fashion as she had arrived and then twisted the British lion's tail again by calling at Diego Garcia. The people on this tiny island outpost had not heard of the outbreak of war, and so they welcomed the *Emden* and permitted her officers and men to relax ashore and carry out minor repairs to the ship. By now the ship had stirred up a hornet's nest with British, Japanese and Russian cruisers searching for her, but still her luck held and she sank four more ships off Ceylon. Von Müller even planned a raid on Penang, the busy port on the west coast of Malaya, where he expected to find a large number of merchantmen.

All through the night of 28 October the *Emden*'s engines drove her towards Penang, at a speed calculated to bring her to the port at dawn. With her dummy funnel rigged she approached the harbour just after 0300 and as she approached the naval anchorage her lookouts made out a string of lights to starboard. They belonged to a guardship, the Russian light cruiser *Jemtchug*, one of the survivors of Tsushima, but her lookouts failed to sound the alarm as the strange cruiser glided closer and closer. At a range of only 300 yards the *Emden* fired a 45cm torpedo from her starboard submerged tube; it ran true and detonated below the Russian's after funnel. The *Jemtchug* valiantly tried to

reply and one gun actually returned the fire, but the *Emden*'s broadsides completed the devastation of the torpedo and as she circled around her opponent her guns poured shells in. A second torpedo finished her off and when the smoke cleared only the *Jemtchug*'s mast was visible.

Von Müller now turned his ship northwards, deciding that it was time to get clear. Still he could not resist the temptation to stop a British merchantman before clearing the harbour, but while his prize crew was boarding the ship the lookouts sighted a strange warship approaching. It was the French destroyer *Mousquet*, determined to try to stop the *Emden*. Although hopelessly outclassed the 300-ton *Mousquet* put up a brave fight before she was overwhelmed by gunfire, and survived only a few minutes.

Now the odds were shortening, for the British and Japanese were determined to catch the *Emden* with their 15 cruisers. Von Müller decided to destroy the cable station in the Cocos-Keeling Islands in the southwestern Pacific. His aims were to destroy the cable and radio station and so interrupt communications between Australia and Great Britain, and to decoy some of the Allied cruisers away from the Indian Ocean. It was apparently his intention to elude his pursuers and slip back into the crowded shipping routes, but this time his luck was out. Although the *Emden*'s radio was tuned to the same frequency as the station at Port Refuge to jam any transmissions, the British operator managed to transmit the fatal words 'Unidentified ship off entrance' before the German landing party started to wreck the installation. Shortly afterwards the *Emden* picked up a transmission from an unknown warship calling the island but as she was estimated to be 250 miles away there seemed to be no need to worry.

But the message had been picked up

Above right: *HMAS* Melbourne, *one of three* Chatham *Class light cruisers built for the new Royal Australian Navy. With the* Sydney *and* Brisbane *she served with the RN for most of World War I.*

Right: *HMS* Antrim, *one of the* Devonshire *Class armoured cruisers built in 1902–05. They were an upgunned version of the original* Kent *or 'County' Class, and saw much war service.*

The French Gueydon *and her sisters were developments from the* Jeanne d'Arc, *on a smaller hull to reduce cost and unhandiness. They proved much more successful and led to the Gloire Class. After a long career as a gunnery training ship the* Gueydon *was finally scuttled at Toulon in 1942.*

by a force of British, Australian and Japanese cruisers escorting a troop-ship convoy, and one of the escorts, the Australian *Sydney* had been detached to investigate. She was only 52 miles away and her plume of smoke was sighted at about 0900 hours, three hours after the *Emden*'s arrival. The Germans were in the worst possible position, taken by surprise with 46 officers and men ashore at the cable station. In his report of the action Captain Glossop remarked on the fact that the *Emden*'s ability to reply at 10,000 yards came as a surprise, but as his own 6-inch guns would have no difficulty in shooting at 14,000 yards this could easily be dealt with. What was even more important was the protection given by the narrow strip of waterline armour which 'entirely defeated' the *Emden*'s 4.1-inch shell at 8000 yards. It was also noted that the German shell seldom burst whereas the *Sydney*'s 6-inch lyddite caused terrible damage. A shell soon destroyed the *Emden*'s radio office and another wiped out the crew of one of the forecastle guns. The fire control system was knocked out and orders had to be passed by voice pipe. By 1045 *Emden*'s fire was becoming feebler

as casualties mounted among the gun crews and ammunition parties. With two funnels demolished and the foremast blown over the ship's side she was rapidly being reduced to a wreck and von Müller decided to run her ashore on North Keeling Island. After a brief respite, when the *Sydney* turned away to catch the escaping collier *Buresk*, the attack on the *Emden* started again. Von Müller wished to surrender to save lives, but all the signal books had been destroyed and it was impossible to reply. After a further five minutes of slaughter someone finally found a white flag and the *Emden*'s ordeal was over. She had lost 134 killed and 65 wounded, against three killed and 13 wounded in the *Sydney*.

The cruise of the *Emden* has never been equalled as an example of cruiser warfare, not only for her success in travelling 30,000 miles and sinking 70,000 tons of shipping, but also for the chivalry and ingenuity of Karl von Müller. By her exploits she disrupted important shipping and tied down a large number of enemy warships. Had she not been unlucky at Cocos Island she might have achieved even more.

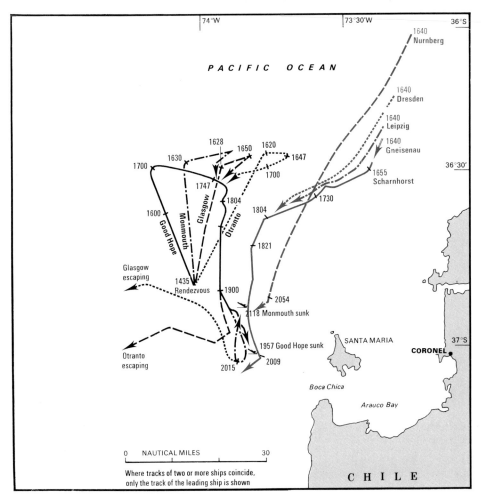

PACIFIC OCEAN

1640 Nurnberg
1640 Dresden
1640 Leipzig
1640 Gneisenau
1655 Scharnhorst

1628 1650 1620 1647
1630 1700
1700 1747
1804 1804 1730
1600 Good Hope Monmouth Glasgow Otranto
1821
Glasgow escaping
1435 Rendezvous 1900
2054
2118 Monmouth sunk
1957 Good Hope sunk
SANTA MARIA
CORONEL
Otranto escaping
2009
2015

Boca Chica
Arauco Bay

0   NAUTICAL MILES   30

Where tracks of two or more ships coincide,
only the track of the leading ship is shown

CHILE

Above: *SMS* Gneisenau, *like her sister*
Scharnhorst, *was built in 1904–08,
and profited from Japanese experience at
Tsushima. The mixture of secondary and
tertiary guns was replaced by six 15cm
and eight 21cm guns, but they were still
rendered obsolete by the battlecruiser.*

Above left: *The Battle of Coronel.*

Left: *The Battle of the Falkland Islands*

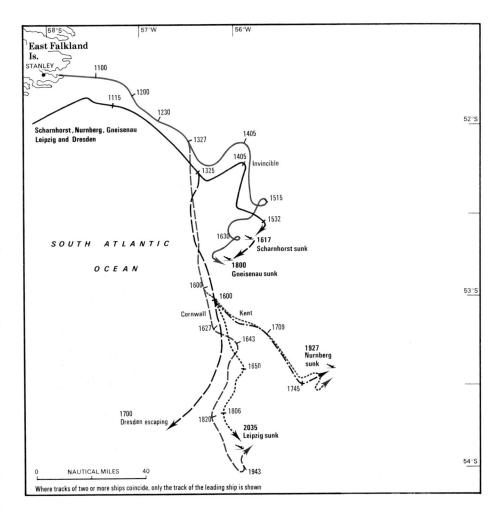

East Falkland Is.
STANLEY
1100
1115 1200
1230
Scharnhorst, Nurnberg, Gneisenau
Leipzig and Dresden
1327 1405
1325 1405
Invincible
1515
1532
1630 **1617** Scharnhorst sunk
1800 Gneisenau sunk

SOUTH ATLANTIC
OCEAN

1600
1600
Cornwall Kent
1627 1709
1643
1650 **1927** Nurnberg sunk
1745
1700 Dresden escaping 1820 1806
2035 Leipzig sunk
1943

0   NAUTICAL MILES   40

Where tracks of two or more ships coincide, only the track of the leading ship is shown

28

The fate of the rest of the Far East Squadron was more dramatic. Vice-Admiral von Spee took his ships to Chilean waters where on 1 November he encountered the British South-East Coast of America Squadron under Rear-Admiral Sir Christopher Cradock. The British squadron included two elderly armoured cruisers, the *Good Hope* and the *Monmouth*, a modern light cruiser HMS *Glasgow* and an armed merchant cruiser, the ex-liner *Otranto*. Six years earlier the *Good Hope* had been the crack gunnery ship of the Channel Fleet, but now she and the *Monmouth* were manned for the most part by reservists and were ill fitted to face the *Scharnhorst* and *Gneisenau*. The British flagship had two single 9.2-inch guns and sixteen 6-inch and the *Monmouth* had fourteen 6-inch; the two German ships were each armed with eight 8.3-inch (21 cm) and six 5.9-inch (15 cm) guns. In theory there was not much to choose between them for speed but the *Monmouth*'s boilers were in poor condition and this would limit the British squadron's speed to 8 knots. Cradock could have called on the battleship *Canopus* but he believed that her speed was no more than 13 knots (on the basis of a very pessimistic report from her engineer). He refused to wait for her to join them from the Falkland Islands.

If Cradock seems rash in his anxiety to court destruction, one must remember certain points. First, the cruise of the *Emden* had shown what havoc could ensue from a well-handled commerce-raiding cruiser. Second, another cruiser-admiral, Troubridge, had just been severely censured for failing to risk his ship in battle against superior forces when HMS *Gloucester* declined to engage the 23,000-ton battlecruiser *Goeben* in the Mediterranean (the Royal Navy sometimes sets impossibly high standards!). Cradock lodged a letter with the British Consul at Valparaiso saying that he would not be accused of any dereliction of duty. A third, and even more valid point, was the possibility of inflicting damage on von Spee's ships. At such a distance from a main base all but the slightest damage would seriously impair a raider's efficiency.

The Battle of Coronel was a one-sided affair. Cradock's ships were silhouetted against the setting sun while von Spee's were difficult to pick out in the fading light, making it impossible to equalise the disparity in gunpower. The chivalrous Cradock ordered the slow armed liner *Otranto* to stay clear of the battle and gave the captain of the light cruiser *Glasgow* discretion to get clear if the squadron was overwhelmed, knowing that her speed would keep her out of trouble. In the grim knowledge that they could not escape, the two British armoured cruisers turned to face the five enemy cruisers. The action began at 1900 as the sun set and an hour later both ships were helpless wrecks, swept by raging fires and they sank with the loss of all hands. By what seemed a miracle the *Glasgow* had escaped with little more than splinter damage, for von Spee's ships had concentrated their fire on the *Good Hope* and *Monmouth*.

Cradock was attacked posthumously for not falling back on the *Canopus*, but the first rule of cruiser warfare is that a commerce-raider has to be attacked when she is located; if von Spee's squadron had disappeared Cradock would have been bitterly criticised for not bringing him to action. Although von Spee's ships had suffered no damage in the battle they had used a lot of ammunition to sink their opponents and this could not be replaced.

Von Spee now decided to attack the tiny British coaling station in the Falkland Islands, on the other side of the continent. To do this he had to take his squadron around Cape Horn, and a photograph taken from one of the light cruisers shows that even to a modern, well-found warship a winter passage 'round the Horn' was a terrifying ordeal. The decision, like that of von Müller to attack the Cocos-Keeling Islands, was a fatal mistake, but in the world of 1914 such gestures counted for a lot and von Spee may also have thought that it was the least expected of all the moves open to him. However the British knew that they had blocked his escape route to the Panama Canal with a powerful Anglo-Japanese squadron, had covered a move back to the Central Pacific with another squadron and had sufficient ships in the South Atlantic to prevent a raid on the River Plate shipping. In all 28 ships were available:

At Suva, Fiji –
1st (Japanese) Squadron, armoured cruisers *Kurama*, *Tsukuba* and *Ikoma*, light cruisers *Chikuma* and *Yahagi*. French armoured cruiser *Montcalm*. British light cruiser HMS *Encounter*.

West Coast of South America –
Australian battlecruiser HMAS *Australia*. Japanese battleship *Hizen* and armoured cruiser *Idzumo*. British light cruiser *Newcastle*.

Off Montevideo –
British battleship HMS *Canopus*, armoured cruisers *Defence*, *Carnarvon*, *Cornwall* and *Kent*, light cruisers *Bristol* and *Glasgow*.

Cape of Good Hope –
British battleship HMS *Albion*, armoured cruiser *Minotaur*, light cruisers *Weymouth*, *Dartmouth*, *Astraea* and *Hyacinth*.

West Indies –
British battlecruiser HMS *Princess Royal*, armoured cruisers *Berwick* and *Lancaster*. French armoured cruiser *Condé*.

Not content with this massive concentration the Admiralty released two battlecruisers from the Grand Fleet, the *Invincible* and *Inflexible*, to be sent to the Falklands to reinforce the cruisers. Correctly divining that von Spee would want to break into the Atlantic for an eventual return to Germany, but also guessing that he would avoid the Panama Canal because it would give away his whereabouts, the British were taking no chances. The battleship *Canopus* was ordered to put herself aground on the mud flats to act as a gun battery in defence of Port Stanley, while some of her light guns were landed to cover the entrance and colliers were hidden in obscure inlets to deny them to the enemy.

The battlecruisers refitted in great haste at Devonport and sailed on 11 November, only 10 days after Coronel, met Admiral Stoddart's cruisers at the Abrolhos Rocks off the coast of Brazil and reached Port Stanley on the night of 7 December. They were just in time, for early next morning at 0800, while the ships were still taking on coal the lookouts on the hills around the harbour entrance reported that von Spee's ships were in sight. It was an anxious moment for the British Admiral, Sturdee, for if von Spee had maintained speed he might have been able to engage the British ships one by one as they came out of the

The British Falmouth *Class ushered in a new generation of seaworthy and well-armed cruisers for work with the Fleet. This 1912 view of HMS* Weymouth *shows how the forward wing 6-inch guns are raised one deck and the midships 6-inch are protected from spray by a light-steel breastwork. In the next class the forecastle deck was carried further aft.*

The wreck of the Königsberg in the Rufiji River in 1915, after being smashed by the 6-inch guns of the British monitors Severn and Mersey. The 10.5cm guns are missing, however, taken ashore to serve with General von Lettow-Vorbeck's army for another three years.

harbour. However the German lookouts, after thinking that the dense clouds of coal smoke might be from the coal supplies being destroyed, spotted the gaunt outline of four tripod masts through the murk. This could only mean dreadnoughts, either battleships or battlecruisers, and von Spee knew that he was doomed.

The *Canopus* fired the first shots, ranging on the *Gneisenau* to discourage her from approaching the harbour, and the two leading German ships immediately turned back to join the rest of the squadron with their terrible news. The armoured cruisers already had steam up and they weighed anchor as fast as they could but it was 1000 before the two battlecruisers could get clear. Only the *Bristol*, which had been carrying out machinery repairs, was left behind with orders to catch up as soon as she could. Von Spee's ships had about 15 miles start but they had been out of dock for some time and their hulls were foul with marine growths; the British settled down to a long stern chase at 20 knots, content to spend the rest of the morning overhauling their prey.

Just before 1300 the *Leipzig* began to drop behind as her stokers began to lose their momentum and the *Inflexible* opened fire on her at 16,000 yards. To try to save his smaller ships von Spee turned back with *Scharnhorst* and *Gneisenau*, giving his light cruisers orders to scatter and leave the big ships to face the pursuers. With a speed advantage of several knots as well as a massive preponderance of gunpower, the two battlecruisers easily prevented the armoured cruisers from closing the range and contented themselves with firing at long range. The result was a long drawn out battering for the *Scharnhorst* before she sank at 1617 while the *Gneisenau* lasted until 1800 hours. Only 200 survivors were saved from the icy waters and many of these died from shock the next day.

The light cruisers had been left to Stoddart; the *Kent* went after the *Nürnberg* while the *Cornwall* and *Glasgow* chased the *Leipzig*, omitting in the confusion to mark the *Dresden*. The 14-year old *Kent* exerted herself to catch the *Nürnberg*, although her claimed feat of reaching 25 knots was an exaggeration, while the *Glasgow* and *Cornwall* had less trouble running down the *Leipzig*. By nightfall von Spee's East Asian Cruiser Squadron was no more, with the *Dresden* taking refuge among the islands of

Above: *The armoured cruiser HMS Bacchante at Mudros in 1915, with the smaller monitor M.32. She provided boats for the Gallipoli landing as well as covering fire from her 9.2-inch and 6-inch guns.*

Tierra del Fuego and the other four cruisers all sunk. The *Bristol* and an armed merchant cruiser rounded up all the German colliers as well to make the victory complete.

The *Dresden* spent the next three months as a fugitive among the forbidding islands of the southernmost tip of South America, helped by local German residents who tipped her off about the presence of enemy ships, but eventually word reached the British. On hearing that she was hiding at the island of Más Afuera (near Juan Fernández, off the coast of Chile) her old enemies HMS *Kent* and *Glasgow* were sent to finish her off. Despite the fact that she was in neutral waters (illegally) the British ships were not prepared to risk her escape and violated Chilean neutrality to get at her. Seeing that escape was impossible her captain scuttled her to avoid capture.

Two more cruisers had been at large, the *Königsberg* and *Karlsruhe*, but on 30 October 1914 it was learned that the *Königsberg* was hiding in the Rufiji River in East Africa. Five days later the *Karlsruhe* sank after a boiler explosion, 200 miles east of Trinidad. The *Königsberg* was swiftly trapped in her lair by the cruiser *Chatham* which ordered two colliers to be sunk across the entrance. Her career as a raider had been brief but eventful; on 20 September 1914 she had caught the smaller cruiser HMS *Pegasus* lying at Zanzibar with her boiler-fires

drawn and had sunk her as easily as the *Emden* had sunk the *Jemtchug* at Penang. She was not finally destroyed until July 1915, by special shallow-draught river monitors sent out from England. Her 4.1-inch guns were put on land-carriages and handed over to General Lettow-Vorbeck, the brilliant commander in East Africa who led British and South African forces a merry chase all over East Africa until 1918.

Mention has already been made of armed merchant cruisers. These were passenger liners provided with guns and commissioned with naval crews. Their primary purpose was to relieve regular cruisers on patrol duties in distant waters. All the major navies had planned for this eventuality for many years, for the high speed of big liners exceeded that of most older cruisers. Merchant ships were not intended to be armed, so it was felt that they would provide easy prey for fast ships armed with six or eight 6-inch guns. In August 1914 the British expected the Germans to send out more than 40 such ships and they themselves requisitioned over 50 liners.

Only five of the German armed liners managed to get to sea, the *Kaiser Wilhelm der Grosse, Cap Trafalgar, Kronprinz Wilhelm, Prinz Eitel Friedrich* and *Berlin*. Three were interned in neutral ports, the *Kaiser Wilhelm der Grosse* was caught off the Rio de Oro in West Africa by the cruiser HMS *Highflyer* and the *Cap Trafalgar* fell in with the British

ex-Cunarder *Carmania* off Trinidad on 14 November 1914. The two 'eggshells armed with hammers' very nearly sank one another but after a fierce gun-duel the *Cap Trafalgar* blew up and sank.

The British used many of their armed merchant cruisers (AMCs) to maintain the Northern Patrol (the famous 10th Cruiser Squadron), a blockading force which patrolled the waters between Scotland and Norway to stop contraband from getting through to Germany. The Germans on the other hand, once their cruisers and armed liners had been swept from the seas, produced a more subtle variation. In 1915-16 a number of cargo-steamers were secretly converted to *hilfskreuzer* (auxiliary cruisers), with concealed guns and torpedo tubes. They were similar to the British Q-Ships in design but instead of trapping submarines their purpose was to look like ordinary tramp steamers, slip through the British and French patrols and then attack commerce in the distant oceans, just as the *Emden* had. In all 13 *hilfskreuzer* were converted, in addition to the original five, and they included the famous names *Greif, Leopard, Wolf, Möwe* and *Seeadler*.

The *Greif* was brought to bay in February 1916 by the British AMCs *Alcantara* and *Andes*, while trying to make her way through the blockade as the Norwegian ship *Rena*. She sank the *Alcantara* but suffered considerable damage herself and while the battle was still

in progress the light cruiser HMS *Comus* and the destroyer *Munster* arrived on the scene. This turned the tables and the raider sank with the loss of 97 lives. The *Leopard* had originally been a British prize taken by the *Möwe* and she was also wearing a Norwegian disguise when she was caught by the armoured cruiser HMS *Achilles* in January 1917. The two most famous raiders were the *Möwe*, which made two cruises under Korvetten-kapitän Burggraf und Graf Nikolaus Zu Dohna-Schlodien and sank 40 ships totalling 180,000 tons, and the sailing barque *Seeadler* which made 15 captures before running aground on a coral reef in the Pacific.

The biggest of the armed merchant cruisers would have been the British liners *Aquitania, Lusitania* and *Mauretania*, which were taken up in August 1914 for conversion. However their coal consumption was enormous and a month later they were returned to the Cunard Company. The persistent story that the *Lusitania* was armed with 6-inch guns when torpedoed in 1915 is based on the original plans to arm her (and other big liners) at the time she was built in 1907. It is ironic that the 'menace' of the big liner on the trade routes, which had haunted naval planners and had inspired the big cruisers in the 1890s, was far surpassed by the achievements of half a dozen tramp steamers and a sailing barque, not one of them capable of more than a moderate speed.

Above: *The Berlin, built in 1902-05, was converted to a minelayer for service in the Baltic in 1915-16 but was then disarmed and hulked. However she came forward from retirement to serve in the truncated German Navy from 1923 to 1935.*

Home Waters 1914-18

While German and Allied cruisers were chasing one another around the trade routes their sisters were in action closer to home. By an exasperating series of errors and misunderstandings the British Mediterranean Fleet let the German battlecruiser *Goeben* slip through their fingers after having her literally in their sights. Rear-Admiral Troubridge, commanding a squadron of four modern armoured cruisers, refused to engage the *Goeben* and the light cruiser *Breslau* on the grounds that his orders prohibited engaging a superior force. Not even the skilful and lengthy pursuit by the light cruisers *Gloucester* and *Dublin* could offset the disgust felt by the Royal Navy for such a paltry excuse; Troubridge's career was ruined, although in fairness he was persuaded by his flag-captain Fawcett Wray against his better judgment. In the light of what happened at the Falklands four months later it is ludicrous to suppose that the *Goeben* and *Breslau* could have picked off the *Defence*, *Warrior*, *Duke of Edinburgh* and *Black Prince*, the two light cruisers and 10 destroyers at will. It is easy to see why Christopher Cradock chose death rather than the dishonour which befell Troubridge and Wray.

Below: *The pursuit of the* Goeben *and the* Breslau *in the Mediterranean.*

The *Goeben* and *Breslau* reached Constantinople in due course and their arrival convinced Turkey that the time was ripe to enter the war on Germany's side. The two ships became *Yavus Sultan Selim* and *Midillie* respectively on 16 August, but continued to be effectively under German control. On 27 October they sortied from the Bosphorus to attack Russian ships and thus dragged Turkey into war with Russia as well. The *Breslau* was used on several occasions as a minelayer and bombarded Russian coastal positions. The Russian Black Sea Fleet was relatively weak but it was handled energetically and cruisers on both sides fought in a number of skirmishes. The new cruisers started just before the war at Nikolaiev were some way away from completion, but after the Turkish light cruiser *Medjidieh* was mined off Odessa the Russians raised her and recommissioned her under the name *Prut*.

In the North Sea events moved equally swiftly. A cruiser, the scout HMS *Amphion*, became the first naval casualty of the war only 13 hours after the outbreak on 5 August, while leading a flotilla of destroyers from Harwich to intercept a mysterious steamer seen 'throwing things overboard'. After sinking the auxiliary minelayer SMS *Königin Luise*, she ran into the minefield laid the previous day. The explosion blew away the *Amphion*'s forecastle and when 20 minutes later a second mine set off the magazine the cruiser sank rapidly.

On 28 August the British took the initiative and sent a powerful force of cruisers and destroyers into the Heligoland Bight to test the German defences. The spearhead was the scout *Fearless* and the new 'light armoured cruiser' *Arethusa*, commissioned only three days before, with 32 destroyers. As intended the German light forces came out to protect their torpedo boats, and soon the *Stettin* and *Frauenlob* were hotly engaging the British forces. The brand-new *Arethusa* was having trouble with her 4-inch guns, which were of a new semi-automatic type, and after receiving 35 hits was reduced to one 6-inch gun. At 1030, when the sweep should have been over, she was still trying to get her guns working and carry out minor machinery repairs. The German light cruiser *Strassburg* loomed out of the mist and for a while it looked as if the *Arethusa* might be sunk, but in the nick of time four 'Town' Class cruisers under Commodore Goodenough arrived and drove off the attackers. But further German reinforcements were hurrying out from the Jade River as fast as the rising tide would

Left: *A 'Town' Class light cruiser at sea in 1917 or 1918. The 'umbrella' spread on the foremast is a baffle to hamper enemy range finding.*

allow and once again the tide of battle swung against the British. Fortunately for them, a destroyer put a torpedo into the light cruiser *Mainz* and then the second batch of re-inforcements arrived, five battlecruisers under Vice-Admiral Sir David Beatty. Their impact on the action was swift, decisive and devastating, the *Köln* and *Ariadne* being sunk in short order and the *Frauenlob*, *Strassburg* and *Stettin* damaged.

The British forces prudently withdrew at this juncture, having taken enough risks for one day, but they had inflicted heavy casualties and suffered comparatively lightly in return. The staffwork had been remarkably inefficient, with Commodores Keyes and Tyrwhitt uninformed about the presence of Goodenough's light cruisers or Beatty's battlecruisers, but the effect on German morale was far-reaching. The Kaiser immediately forbade any sorties which might lead to losses and the Naval Staff was forced to acquiesce to a defensive policy, in total opposition to all that they had been taught before the war. The result was that British light forces gained the ascendancy in the North Sea.

The Harwich Force, comprising light cruisers and destroyers under Commodore Reginald Tyrwhitt, was stationed in the southern part of the North Sea to guard against any attempt by the High Seas Fleet to enter the English Channel. From August 1914 a constant stream of soldiers and supplies passed across the Channel to France and the British knew how vulnerable this supply-line was to surface attack. The Harwich Force was charged with the task of protecting the Southern flank and Tyrwhitt interpreted this to mean that offence was the best form of defence. His forces were con-

stantly on the move, in all weathers, and although the rate of attrition was high German surface forces throughout the four years of war were only able to sink one empty transport in the Channel.

A Royal Navy destroyer-captain, Lieutenant-Commander Taprell Dorling (later famous as the author *Taffrail*), left a vivid description of a sortie by the Harwich Force in 1915. The operation was to cover an attempt to fly off seaplanes from two seaplane carriers to bomb the island of Borkum. On this particular morning the early fine weather rapidly turned to fog and the *Arethusa* hoisted the 'Negative' signal to abort the mission. The whole force, some 30 ships in tight formation, was rapidly swallowed up in the murk, but still maintained course at 20 knots, steering by compass and watching the wake of the ship ahead. The *Arethusa*'s siren signalled in Morse for all to reduce speed to 10 knots and each ship in turn repeated the longs and shorts; then another burst of signals ordered a turn in succession eight points (90 degrees) to starboard. Within minutes the three columns of ships were bunching, unable to see the next ahead. Suddenly there was a terrible noise of grinding steel, followed by shouting; the destroyer *Landrail* had run into the light cruiser *Undaunted*, cutting a deep V-shaped gash on the port side aft. The light cruiser, second of the *Arethusa* Class, was badly damaged but would probably be able to limp back to port, but the destroyer was in a poor way with 20 feet of her forecastle crushed and almost destroyed. To make matters worse the whole force of light cruisers

and destroyers was now in confusion, milling around in the fog and increasing the chances of more collisions.

The Harwich Force was only 10-12 miles from Borkum, well inside the Heligoland Bight and easily intercepted by German light forces. In 1915 there was still no real awareness of the need to keep strict radio silence. There could be no doubt that the Germans were aware that something was going on and that ships nearby were acknowledging signals from a shore station. But Commodore Tyrwhitt was not the man to abandon a ship or her men, and while the *Undaunted* slowly got under way with an escort of two destroyers and the seaplane carriers were sent home, the *Arethusa* and her sister *Aurora* turned back to find the *Landrail*. The weather was deteriorating and it looked more and more likely that the destroyer would have to be abandoned, but after 71 hours of back-breaking labour the *Arethusa* towed her into Harwich.

Action with the light cruisers and destroyers could be a terrifying and hectic business and the outcome was largely a matter of luck. There was the constant risk of being torpedoed, the hidden menace of mines and the constant hazards of operating in close formation at high speed. Tyrwhitt's flagship, the *Arethusa*, came to grief in February 1916 in a newly-laid minefield off Harwich and although the sturdy little cruiser did not sink, the tow parted in rough weather, allowing her to drift onto a shoal off Felixstowe. Eventually she

Right: Calliope, *and her sister HMS* Champion, *marked the first departure from the basic Arethusa/Caroline design. Boiler improvements permitted the reduction from three to two funnels and in 1916 it proved possible to re-arm them with four 6-inch guns and provide director control on a tripod foremast.*

Above: *HMS* Birmingham, *showing an unusual variety of range-finder baffles, triangular brackets on three funnels.*

Below: *HMS* Aurora, *second of the Arethusa Class, in August 1914. The improvements introduced in the Calliope were extended to the earlier classes and the Arethusas received a tripod mast and three 6-inch guns.*

broke her back and had to be written off as a total loss. Tyrwhitt transferred his broad pennant to the newer light cruiser *Cleopatra* and was back in action almost immediately. Towards the end of March 1916 four light cruisers and the destroyers escorted another seaplane carrier in an attempt to bomb the Zeppelin sheds at Tondern, on the mainland behind the island of Sylt. The following night the captain of the *Cleopatra* sighted a ship steaming past on the port bow and realised from the sparks billowing out of her funnels that she was a coal-burner and therefore German. Increasing speed the cruiser turned to starboard and suddenly two destroyers appeared across her bows. The *Cleopatra* rammed the second destroyer, the German *G.194*, cutting her in two while the next astern, the *Undaunted*, opened fire with her 6-inch and 4-inch guns. The German destroyer suffered a horrible fate; the forward half continued to rush forward in a shower of sparks and steam, with the men on board screaming, but no survivors were found.

The *Arethusa* type of cruiser, with its destroyer-type machinery, proved ideally fast and manoeuvrable for close-range action of this kind and the following class, the *Carolines*, were very similar. Their only weak point was the mixed armament and this was soon changed. Five of the *Arethusa*s were given an extra 6-inch amidships and all received two extra pairs of torpedo tubes. The *Caroline*s had started with a pair of 4-inch guns forward and both 6-inch guns aft and this idiosyncratic disposition soon gave way to a third 6-inch on the forecastle, but in time a fourth 6-inch was mounted amidships as in the early ships.

This was a more sensible arrangement, and so the seventh and eighth of the *Caroline* Class were completed this way in the second half of 1915. They also adopted a different arrangement of boilers, which allowed the three funnels to be reduced to two and gave more deck space. Here was a balanced design still on a modest displacement and so another

Below: *SMS* Blücher *was the last German armoured cruiser. She was laid down in 1907 before news of the British battlecruisers' design was fully appreciated. Despite her inferior protection she was risked at the Dogger Bank battle in January 1915, and paid the price.*

Right: *HMS* Centaur *in the Black Sea in 1919. She and the* Concord *mark a step forward from the* Calliope *and* Castor *Classes, with a fifth 6-inch gun between the tripod mast and the funnels.*

four, known as the *Cambrian* Class, were
started at the end of 1914. Two sets of
turbines for a pair of Turkish scout
cruisers were acquired from Vickers (the
ships had not been laid down) and they
were used for two more ships of slightly
enlarged type, the *Centaur* and *Concord*.
On the same length as the *Cambrian* and
only a slight increase in beam it was
possible to squeeze in a fifth 6-inch. The
Centaur showed how tough she was by
surviving two minings and losing her
bow and stern, and the design was
repeated in the four *Caledon* Class laid
down early in 1916. In all three wartime
developments of the original *Arethusa/
Caroline* type the 4-inch secondary gun
was discarded, and because of this 'all-big
gun' concept they were nicknamed
'Tyrwhitt's Dreadnoughts'.

The development of the type did not
stop there for the British now realised
that too many changes in design would
slow down the building rate. The five
Ceres Class were similar to the *Caledons*
but with a sensible re-arrangement of
the guns. Instead of the clumsy position
for the fifth 6-inch gun, between the
bridge and the foremost funnel, the
superstructure was moved back and the
extra gun was raised a deck to fire over
the forward 6-inch. The extra top-

Above: *German light-cruiser design
belatedly followed the British lead in
adopting a uniform armament of 15cm
guns. The* Karlsruhe, *completed in
December 1916, was armed with eight
15cm guns and steamed at 27.5 knots.
She is seen here at Scapa Flow in
November 1918.*

Below: *The* Dresden *belonged to the
second group of war-built German light
cruisers, but they differed only in details
from the new* Königsberg *Class. Note
the heavy armament of two 60cm
(23.6-inch) torpedo tubes on either beam
and the heavy gun armament.*

weight was balanced by another increase in beam and the sum total was a great improvement. The main drawback was common to the whole series, extreme wetness forward, and a further five ships (the *Calcutta* Class) laid down at the end of 1917 cured this by having a raised or 'trawler' bow. For some reason the 'C' names of the *Caroline* Class had been continued and the whole series were known collectively as the 'C' Class, despite the considerable variations in size and armament.

The design went through one more permutation. Between September 1916 and March 1918 an enlarged type was started, with 20 feet more length and 2 feet 6 inches more beam to allow a sixth 6-inch gun to be mounted. Unfortunately the only place to put it was between the bridge and the forefunnel, the very place that had been found undesirable in the *Centaur* and *Caledon* designs, and so the increase in armament was no great improvement, but the increase in dimensions made them more seaworthy. As with the *Ceres* and *Calcutta* Classes, the second batch was given 'trawler' bows to cure the wetness in a head sea. Work proceeded slowly on these ships, however, and the first were not ready until the last months of the war.

Across the North Sea the Germans also built cruisers for the North Sea although the growing emphasis on U-Boat construction meant that the tempo was not maintained. The trend set in the last pre-war design, the *Frankfurt* and *Wiesbaden*, for a uniform armament of 5.9-inch guns, was maintained. A new class started in 1914 was given the names of older cruisers sunk in 1914: *Königsberg*, *Emden*, *Karlsruhe* and *Nürnberg*. They were good-looking three-funnellers with an armament approximating that of the British 'Towns', eight 5.9-inch, but their speed with mixed coal- and oil-fired boilers was 27-28 knots, close to the *Arethusa*'s. A similar class of 10 ships was planned to follow, but only the new *Dresden* and *Köln* were commissioned by the end of the war.

The only other cruisers to join the High Seas Fleet were four ships which owed their existence to Russian plans for expansion. The *Muraviev Amursky* and *Nevelskoy* were similar to the new *Königsberg* Class, and were building at the Danzig yard of Schichau. Both were seized immediately after the outbreak of war and became SMS *Pillau* and SMS *Elbing*. At the same time work stopped on four sets of steam turbines for a Russian battlecruiser and only as an afterthought was a new design drawn up to make use of this powerful machinery. Two fast minelaying cruisers were built, the *Bremse* and *Brummer*, each driven by two 23,500hp turbines at a speed of 28 knots. As they were intended to operate in enemy waters a strong resemblance to the *Arethusa* Class was fostered, with three slim funnels, a graceful clipper stem and a collapsible mainmast. Their capacious upper deck stowed 400 mines and they carried an armament similar to the British *Cambrian* Class, with four 5.9-inch guns.

The bigger and therefore more weatherly 'Town' Class light cruisers served with the Grand Fleet and were based at its bleak anchorage in Scapa Flow in the Orkneys, or with the battlecruisers in the Firth of Forth. One of them, the *Birmingham*, was escorting battleships after a gunnery practice on 9 August 1914 when she saw a U-Boat on the surface. It was *U.15*, apparently immobilised by a machinery breakdown, and the cruiser carved through her at about 20 knots; it was the first U-Boat to be sunk. Little over a month later *U.9* took an ample revenge by sinking the old armoured cruisers *Aboukir*, *Cressy* and *Hogue* within the space of an hour. The

disaster was unnecessary for these vulnerable ships had been left to patrol a fixed line without even a single destroyer to escort them. The same U-Boat sank the old 1st Class cruiser *Hawke* off Aberdeen on 15 October, demonstrating how much more destructive the current generation of torpedoes were when compared with the 14-inch type in use when the late-Victorian cruisers were designed.

The Battle of the Dogger Bank, fought on 23 January 1915, showed that even a big modern armoured cruiser like the German *Blücher* had no hope of standing up to capital ships' guns. The British light cruisers, although excluded from the main action by their light armament, played their part in scouting for the battlecruisers, with the *Aurora* making the first sighting report and the *Arethusa* helping to finish off the badly damaged *Blücher*. It was a classic example of how light cruisers could stiffen a destroyer attack, for the *Blücher*'s guns had crippled the leading British destroyer, HMS *Meteor*, with five hits; the *Arethusa* arrived with the rest of the Harwich Force destroyers and used her 6-inch guns to divert attention from the *Meteor* and cover the final torpedo attack which sank the German cruiser.

The Battle of Jutland on 31 May 1916 saw cruisers functioning just as they had been intended to, scouting for the battle fleet and leading destroyers in attacks against the enemy battle line. There were no fewer than 34 cruisers of all kinds on the British side and 11 on the German side:

Below: *HMS* Canterbury, *one of the* Castor Class. *They were initially armed with two 6-inch guns aft, 4-inch guns on the forecastle and 4-inch amidships. In 1916 all four ships were given a uniform armament of four 6-inch guns.*

Above: *The German light cruiser* Pillau *survived heavy damage in the night action at Jutland and in 1920 was handed over to the Italians as reparations. Under her new name* Bari *she lasted until 1943 when American bombs sank her at Leghorn.*

Grand Fleet

1st Cruiser Squadron	– *Defence, Warrior, Duke of Edinburgh, Black Prince.*
2nd Cruiser Squadron	– *Minotaur, Hampshire, Cochrane, Shannon.*
4th Light Cruiser Squadron	– *Calliope, Constance, Caroline, Royalist, Comus.*
Attached to Grand Fleet Battlecruisers	– *Boadicea, Blanche, Bellona, Active, Canterbury, Chester.*
Leading 11th Destroyer Flotilla	– *Castor.*

Battle Cruiser Fleet

1st Light Cruiser Squadron	– *Galatea, Phaeton, Inconstant, Cordelia.*
2nd Light Cruiser Squadron	– *Southampton, Birmingham, Nottingham, Dublin.*
3rd Light Cruiser Squadron	– *Falmouth, Yarmouth, Birkenhead, Gloucester.*
Leading 1st Destroyer Flotilla	– *Fearless.*
Leading 13th Destroyer Flotilla	– *Champion.*

High Seas Fleet

Fourth Scouting Group	– *Stettin, München, Hamburg, Frauenlob, Stuttgart.*
Flagship of Torpedo Boat Flotillas	– *Rostock.*

Battlecruiser Force

Flagship of Torpedo Boat Flotillas	– *Regensburg.*
2nd Scouting Group	– *Frankfurt, Wiesbaden, Pillau, Elbing.*

All three types of cruiser were present on the British side, the big armoured cruisers acting as a heavy scouting wing of the Grand Fleet, the light cruisers and even four scouts attached to the battle squadrons. The Germans on the other hand, with only a few elderly armoured cruisers, had only light cruisers with the High Seas Fleet.

Inevitably the first sighting was made by cruisers. A lookout in HMS *Galatea*, flagship of the 1st Light Cruiser Squadron, sighted a ship blowing off steam. It was a Danish steamer and as she was in between the outer wing of each fleet she was in view of the German cruiser *Elbing*. After months of fruitless sorties and sweeps there was a noticeable exhilaration when the signal 'Enemy in Sight' was hoisted to the cruisers' mastheads. Pausing only to exchange shots the two forces turned away to rejoin their fleets and the only full-scale fleet action of the war was about to begin.

First blood went to the *Elbing*, with a hit below the *Galatea*'s bridge, but it failed to explode and Commodore Alexander Sinclair's flagship turned away to try to entice the 2nd Scouting Group northwards. His aim was to lead the whole enemy fleet (and nobody knew how big it was) north, allowing Vice-Admiral Beatty and the battlecruisers to get between it and its bases. However laudable the aim of cutting off the Germans might have been, the 1st Light Cruiser Squadron was failing in its first duty, that of forcing its way past the German cruiser screen to find out just what size of main force it was screening. Until that information was available Beatty could form no battle plan and the Commander-in-Chief, Admiral Jellicoe, who was at sea with the Grand Fleet, could not co-ordinate movements with his subordinate. So for the moment Beatty had to content himself with trying to engage Rear-Admiral Boedicker's 2nd Scouting Group, in ignorance of the fact that Vice-Admiral Hipper and his battlecruisers were coming up in support at 25 knots. The German scouting had been more methodical, but the *Elbing* had reported the British three-funnelled light cruisers as battlecruisers, and a further report from her about recognition signals had been misinterpreted as a sighting of 24 or 26 battleships! Thus Hipper was in receipt of muddling information at the outset of the battle, and had no knowledge of the actual whereabouts of either Beatty or Jellicoe.

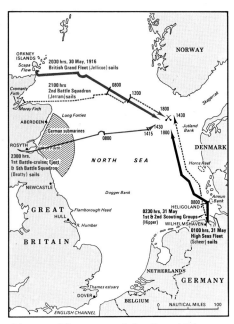

Above: *The routes of the Grand Fleet and High Seas Fleet before Jutland.*

At 1529 *Galatea* caught sight of five columns of heavy smoke behind the pursuing German light cruisers, and interpreting them correctly as major warships steaming at maximum speed signalled the course and bearing to Beatty. At 1548 the first shots were fired and it was time for the light cruisers to draw clear, leaving the giants to fight it out. In the first phase the German ships scored first and when the *Indefatigable* blew up under heavy fire from the *von der Tann*, Beatty ordered the light cruiser *Champion* and her flotilla of destroyers to make a torpedo attack on the enemy to relieve the pressure. In the meantime the battle was swinging back in Beatty's favour, as his four powerful

fast battleships of the *Queen Elizabeth* Class had come up in support. Despite the loss of a second battlecruiser, HMS *Queen Mary*, the concentrated salvoes of 13.5-inch and 15-inch shells were scoring more and more hits. On his own initiative Commodore Heinrich in the light cruiser *Regensburg* ordered his own destroyers and torpedo boats to attack Beatty's line and take the pressure off Hipper.

The two light cruisers could do little more than fire in support of the lean, black-painted torpedo craft as they raced forward through a vicious cross-fire from the secondary guns of both sides' battlecruisers. No hits were made by torpedoes on either side, although the more powerfully armed British destroyers drove off the Germans with the loss of two boats and then suffered the disablement of two of their own.

In contrast to the 1st Light Cruiser Squadron's misguided attempt at trailing its coat the 2nd Cruiser Squadron under Commodore William Goodenough showed how light cruisers were meant to perform their job. Regardless of the danger, Goodenough pressed on southwards until at 1633 he succeeded in closing to within 13,000 yards of the main High Seas Fleet under Vice-Admiral Scheer, 22 battleships and their attendant destroyers. As Goodenough kept his ships bows on they were mistaken at first for friendly ships at that great distance, but as soon as the four 'Towns' turned away their unmistakable four funnels revealed them to be British and a hurricane of 11-inch and 12-inch shells

smothered them. But the four cruisers zig-zagged and weaved their way through the 200-foot high splashes to safety, all the while sending out the vital signal, 'Have sighted enemy battle fleet, bearing southeast. Enemy's course north. My position 56 degrees 34 seconds north, 6 degrees 20 minutes east', followed 10 minutes later by fuller details of numbers and types of ships.

Goodenough was only two miles ahead of the *Lion*, Beatty's flagship, when he made his momentous sighting, and so it was only a matter of minutes before the admiral could see for himself. Secure in the knowledge that his own Commander-in-Chief was in support, he now turned his battlecruisers and battleships through 180 degrees and headed northwest, with Scheer and Hipper now in pursuit. The Grand Fleet was disposed in cruising order with six columns of four dreadnoughts each, the 4th Light Cruiser Squadron and the destroyers forming an anti-submarine screen and the armoured cruisers of the 1st and 2nd Cruiser Squadrons eight miles ahead as a scouting screen. These big ships had been stationed eight miles apart, forming a 40-mile wide 'hay rake' to provide the maximum chance of sighting the enemy but as the visibility decreased through the afternoon the distance had been halved to maintain visual contact. In addition Jellicoe had pushed his 3rd Battlecruiser Squadron under Rear-Admiral Hood 20 miles ahead to provide a rapid re-inforcement for Beatty as soon as contact was made. With Hood were seven light cruisers. It

Left: *The opening phase of Jutland, the battlecruisers' engagement.*

Below: *The engagement of the main fleets at Jutland.*

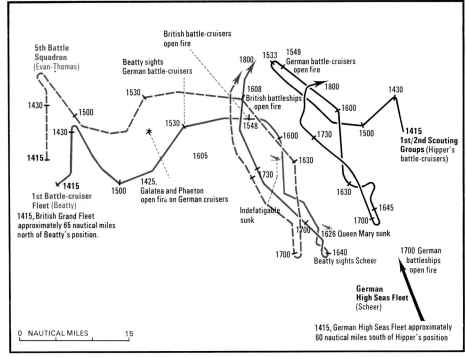

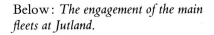

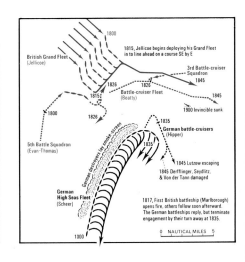

must be remembered that without aerial reconnaissance or any aid but the human eye, scouting was the hardest job of all and visual contact was essential.

Precise news was just what Jellicoe did not get, for apart from Goodenough, none of the subordinate commanders seem to have understood the need to signal precise bearings and courses of any ships sighted. The reliance on the flagship and the senior officer present to make all situation reports was no doubt intended to avoid a plethora of contradictory reports, but by 1600 on 31 May 1916, the *Lion*'s radio equipment had been shot away, she was belching clouds of black smoke which made flag or lamp signals impossible to read and was in any case under heavy fire and firing herself. After several attempts at getting coherent reports out of the battlecruisers, Goodenough's positive sighting and detailed information came as a refreshing change. At 1630 two cruisers made contact at last, the *Falmouth* of Beatty's 3rd Light Cruiser Squadron and the armoured cruiser *Black Prince* of Jellicoe's 1st Cruiser Squadron. But once again the reports were couched in terms which were, to say the least, unhelpful. *Falmouth* told *Black Prince*, 'Battlecruisers engaged to the south south-west of me', which *Black Prince* relayed as 'Enemy battlecruisers bearing south five miles'. What the *Falmouth* had not mentioned was that she was reporting British battlecruisers, not German, but as the message took some time to reach the flagship Jellicoe's staff were able to deduce that a mix-up had occurred. Even the admirable Goodenough fell into a common trap when at 1750 he gave a bearing which was a 180 degree reciprocal of the correct one; in the heat

of battle such confusion happens but some of the reports of the other commanders at Jutland can only be termed sloppy and inadequate. All the time visibility was decreasing, with funnel-smoke from some 200 coal-burning ships adding to the miasma.

The final deployment and engagement between the two fleets are too well known to be described here, but in the preliminary stages of Jellico's masterly resolution of the confused situation an important cruiser engagement occurred. As we have already seen, Admiral Hood's three battlecruisers had been pushed ahead of the Grand Fleet to improve the likelihood of bringing the High Seas Fleet to action. This was the sort of work the battlecruisers should have done all along, rather than fight in line like dreadnoughts, and Hood thought more like a cruiser admiral than a battle-fleet commander. With the light cruisers *Canterbury* and *Chester* five miles ahead and to starboard he was hoping to meet Beatty's battlecruisers but as a result of a dead-reckoning error made by the *Lion* he was much closer to Hipper's ships, which were 12 miles away but hidden by mist.

The *Chester* heard heavy gunfire to the southwest and when she turned to investigate she ran into Admiral Boedicker's 2nd Scouting Group of four light cruisers at a range of little more than three miles. She was a new ship, little more than a month out of the builder's yard and she was immediately deluged by a rain of shells without making an effective reply. Showers of shell splinters scythed down her gun crews, although luckily nothing vital was hit and she was able to claw her way clear of the trap and escape. Her agony had been exacerbated because she had been designed for the Greeks with a new type of 5.5-inch gun, whose shield did not extend all the way down to the deck as in the Royal Navy's 6-inch. As a result the hail of splinters had swept under the shields and three-quarters of the wounds reported were below the knee. One eye witness remembered the ghastly sight of rows of wounded lying in the ammunition passages, minus their feet. Yet these indomitable men were wisecracking with one another, unaware that they would be dead within hours from shock and loss of blood.

The embodiment of the *Chester*'s spirit was Boy 1st Class Jack Cornwell, who had been a sight-setter and communications number on one of the guns. The rest of the crew had been knocked out and he himself had been mortally wounded by a splinter, yet this 16-year-old remembered his orders and waited at his gun for orders which never came.

Below: *The light cruiser* Chester *was roughly handled by German light cruisers at Jutland. She is seen here in 1917, after her pole foremast had been replaced by a tripod supporting the director control for her 5.5-inch guns.*

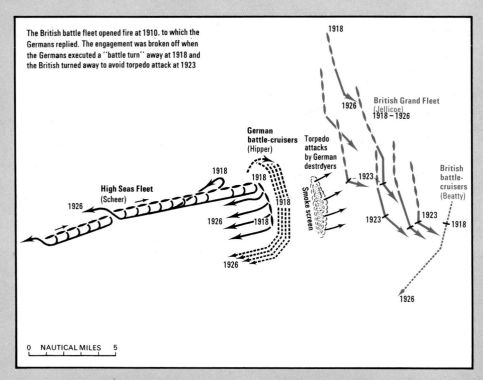

The British battle fleet opened fire at 1910, to which the Germans replied. The engagement was broken off when the Germans executed a "battle turn" away at 1918 and the British turned away to avoid torpedo attack at 1923

High Seas Fleet (Scheer)

German battle-cruisers (Hipper)

Torpedo attacks by German destroyers

Smoke screen

British Grand Fleet (Jellicoe) 1918–1926

British battle-cruisers (Beatty)

0 NAUTICAL MILES 5

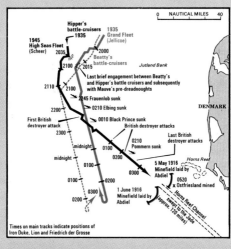

0 NAUTICAL MILES 40

Hipper's battle-cruisers 1935

1935 Grand Fleet (Jellicoe)

1945 High Seas Fleet (Scheer)

2000 Beatty's battle-cruisers

Jutland Bank

Last brief engagement between Beatty's and Hipper's battle cruisers and subsequently with Mauve's pre-dreadnoughts

DENMARK

2245 Frauenlob sunk

0210 Elbing sunk

First British destroyer attack

0010 Black Prince sunk

British destroyer attacks

midnight

0210 Pommern sunk

Last British destroyer attacks

midnight

5 May 1916 Minefield laid by Abdiel

Horns Reef

0520 x Ostfriesland mined

1 June 1916 Minefield laid by Abdiel

Horns Reef Channel swept to the Jade approx. 120 miles

Times on main tracks indicate positions of Iron Duke, Lion and Friedrich der Grosse

Above: *Admiral Scheer's escape after Jutland, when the High Seas Fleet battered its way through Jellicoe's light cruisers and destroyers.*

Left: *The 'battle turnaway' of the High Seas Fleet.*

Below: *HMS* Birmingham, *heavily engaged during a fierce night action against German light cruisers at Jutland, suffered no casualties but her funnels and upperworks were riddled with splinters.*

When the stretcher-parties found him he was still at his post, headphones on and adjusting the sights. The boy survived long enough to be taken ashore to a naval hospital, but died soon after from his wound and has since been immortalised as the Royal Navy's youngest holder of the Victoria Cross.

The German cruisers were quickly punished when Hood's battlecruisers came storming out of the mist. The *Wiesbaden* was shattered by 12-inch shells and came to a stop, while the *Pillau* had four boilers put out of action and a fire started in her stokeholds which killed and wounded many men. The survivors of the 2nd Scouting Group fled, baffled by the appearance of capital ships from an unexpected quarter. Understandably Boedicker concluded that he had run into the main British Fleet and so did Commodore Heinrich, who launched his torpedo boats in an attack. A wild *mêlée* resulted, but again the attack failed and the Germans fell back to regroup.

A second cruiser epic was now about to unfold. The crippled *Wiesbaden* lay between the opposing lines of ships and she was fired on in turn by the British ships as they passed. The destroyer *Onslow*, for example, fired 58 shells into her while the 3rd Light Cruiser Squadron poured 6-inch shells into her as they passed, but still she refused to surrender and her guns fired intermittently. Then Rear-Admiral Sir Robert Arbuthnot's 1st Cruiser Squadron came into view, crossing the bows of the *Lion* in its haste to get at the *Wiesbaden*. Once again the treacherous visibility allowed ships to get surprisingly close and while the *Defence*, *Warrior* and *Black Prince* were briskly pouring salvoes of 9.2-inch shells into the blazing hulk they were surprised by the German battlecruisers and the 3rd Battle Squadron. The *Warrior* was quickly set on fire, but the fate of the *Defence* was the same as the *Indefatigable* and *Queen Mary*; there was a sudden ripple of explosions as the cordite charges in her fore and aft ammunition passages detonated, a giant explosion and only a pall of smoke to mark her grave. The *Warrior* might have followed her flagship but for the intervention of the battleship *Warspite*, whose helm had jammed as she was manoeuvring to take up her position astern of the main fleet. Tempted by the choice of a new battleship rather than a mere cruiser the German ships shifted target and the crippled *Warrior* gratefully limped away.

Once the main fleets engaged the hard-worked cruisers and torpedo craft could go back to maintaining a watch, but once the German Fleet had executed its two 180 degree turns and had finally disengaged, it fell to the light forces to again maintain contact and provide information. The resulting night action of the Battle of Jutland was, if anything, more savage than the day fighting which had just finished. But before night fell the indomitable *Wiesbaden* scored a final success by torpedoing the British dreadnought *Marlborough* in the engine-room. As the *Wiesbaden* sank with all hands later that night, we will never know what heroism it took to get that torpedo tube trained and fired. Her 589 officers and men went to an unmarked grave having fought their ship almost literally to the last shell.

In the fading twilight HMS *Castor*, flagship of the 11th Destroyer Flotilla and the *Calliope*, *Comus* and *Constance* of the 4th Light Cruiser Squadron skirmished with the German 3rd Squadron of battleships while chasing some torpedo boats, but their message to Jellicoe failed to give any details. At 2010 the 3rd Light Cruiser Squadron engaged the 4th Scouting Group and hit the *München*, but soon lost contact without giving any range, course or bearing to the Commander-in-Chief. The most tantalising chance of all was presented to the *Caroline* and *Royalist* when at 2045 they sighted three of the German 1st Squadron; just as they turned to attack with torpedoes Vice-Admiral Jerram of the 2nd Battle Squadron convinced himself that they were British ships and countermanded the attack. At a range of only 10,000 yards the British ships would have wrought great execution and the gunfire would have brought reinforcements immediately, but the German and British battle squadrons parted without firing a shot at one another. When the two light cruisers finally persuaded the cautious admiral to allow an attack the moment had passed and their torpedoes missed.

The situation at the end of this daylight phase of the battle was that the two fleets were out of touch but proceeding roughly southwards parallel to one another. The British were steaming slightly faster to ensure that they would still be between the High Seas Fleet and its bases at daylight, and left their light cruisers and destroyers astern to guard against any German attempt to force their way around behind the fleet.

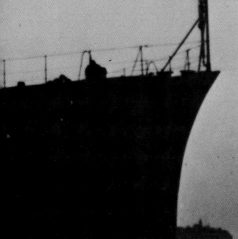

Jellicoe was very wary of fighting a night action, for he rightly felt that the risks of friendly ships being attacked far outweighed any advantage he might gain. Given the scattered forces and the primitive communications available in 1916 it was a reasonable conclusion, but the Germans had reached a different one. They had assiduously practised night fighting and in any case dared not face the Grand Fleet in the morning. It was a matter of desperation as much as any confidence in his fleet's skill that decided Scheer to risk crossing astern of Jellicoe's main fleet. He was also aided by an unexpected windfall. At about 2130 the *Lion*, whose signal books had been destroyed in the battle, asked her consort *Princess Royal* to provide the night challenge and reply. This was passed by flashing lamp 'in clear', but what the British did not know was that the signal had been seen by light cruisers of the 2nd and 4th Scouting Groups, hiding in the mist only two miles away. Before they turned away they had intercepted the correct challenge, although they had not had time to observe the reply.

Throughout the night engagements which followed British ships held their fire for a fatal few seconds because they were challenged correctly. Conversely the Germans knew that any ship challenging could be fired on immediately. The first ship to suffer this treatment was the light cruiser *Castor*, which was roughly handled by the *Hamburg* and *Elbing* when she mistook them for friendly ships.

Characteristically Goodenough's 2nd Light Cruiser Squadron avoided this confusion by correctly interpreting the significance of the gun-flashes of the *Castor*'s engagement, and all four cruisers were ready when they ran into the 4th Scouting Group. The distance came down steadily from 1500 yards to 800 before the Germans gave their own challenge, unable to stand the strain. Immediately the *Dublin* fired a 6-inch shell into one of the black shapes and she and the *Southampton* switched on their searchlights. A murderous fight ensued, with both sides firing rapidly and shells bursting everywhere. Shell splinters caused terrible casualties on the *Southampton*'s open deck and both she and the *Dublin* were soon ablaze. The two ships astern, the *Nottingham* and *Birmingham*, kept their searchlights switched off and

pumped shells into the German cruisers without suffering any casualties. So great was the uproar that when the *Southampton* fired a torpedo from her submerged torpedo tube nobody on the bridge heard the explosion. But as if by a miracle the searchlights went out and the firing stopped. It was the *Frauenlob*, which had broken in two and sunk with the loss of 323 men, and the rest of her squadron vanished into the night.

The *Southampton*, like her near-sister *Chester*, had suffered grievously from splinter damage, with 35 killed and 55 wounded, and her entire upperworks were riddled with holes. She had been hit 18 times but damage to hull and machinery was superficial. Her sister *Dublin* was hit 13 times but had much lighter casualties. With her navigating officer dead and all charts destroyed she lost contact with her squadron during the night and did not find them until daybreak.

When the German battleships crashed through the destroyer screen similar scenes were repeated. The armoured cruiser *Black Prince*, which had last been heard of attacking the *Wiesbaden*, suddenly blundered into the German battle line and was obliterated in an explosion

as battleship after battleship riddled her at point-blank range. In the confusion caused by British destroyers' attacks the light cruiser *Elbing* weaved and dodged through the battle line and failed to make it; she was run down by the battleship *Posen* and had to be abandoned. The *Rostock* nearly succeeded in the same manoeuvre, but took a torpedo in the boiler-room as she slid through a gap between two battleships; she too had to be abandoned.

Jutland (or Skagerrak to the Germans) was tactically indecisive but cruisers on both sides showed that they were much tougher than anyone had claimed. On the other hand, the original British battlecruisers showed only too clearly that they had been cast in the wrong role. Like the *Defence*, on whose design they had been based, the *Invincible* and *Indefatigable* could not hope to engage battleships in a slugging match and they paid the price. On the other hand ships like the *Chester, Southampton* and *Wiesbaden* survived very heavy attack. Time and again the light cruisers provided the extra muscle which destroyers lacked, at the same time being small enough to be risked and tough enough to take punishment. Of all the ship types which were tested at Jutland the light cruiser emerged as the most satisfactory, and it is significant that only three were sunk by torpedoes and gunfire, the *Wiesbaden, Frauenlob* and *Rostock*.

Below: *SMS* Köln *running trials at the end of 1917. British cruisers tended to make less smoke when steaming fast because they used Welsh 'steam' coal (anthracite), a factor which sometimes made a vital difference in scouting.*

After Jutland

One clear result of Jutland was confirmation of the value of the light cruiser as a fleet scout and a stiffener for destroyer attacks. Nothing could be done for the moment about the vulnerability of gun crews to shrapnel and shell splinters, for the 'Town', *Arethusa* and 'C' Classes were all too small for turret mountings, but note was taken for the future. What did improve was fire control and communications.

At Jutland the seaplane carrier *Engadine* had launched a seaplane to scout for the Grand Fleet and although the vital message had not been sent because of a radio failure, there were hopes that aircraft might provide better reconnaissance. Another requirement was to prevent the Germans from getting their reconnaissance from the giant Zeppelins which regularly gave away the position of British squadrons and enabled the Germans to avoid action. In June 1917 a platform was installed on the forecastle of HMS *Yarmouth* to test the theory of a naval aviator, Flight Commander Rutland, that he could fly a Sopwith Pup fighter from a 20-foot runway. If this proved feasible cruisers could not only launch aircraft to deal with the Zeppelin nuisance but also to investigate suspicious ships. The experiment was a great success and a short while after the first take-offs another pilot took off from the *Yarmouth* and shot down a Zeppelin.

Two forms of platform were approved for light cruisers, a standard one over the forward gun with screens to protect the fragile aircraft, and a more sophisticated type which could revolve to point the aircraft into the wind. Bow platforms were fitted to a large number of light cruisers of the 'Town', *Arethusa* and 'C' Classes, while a few of the later 'C' Class received the revolving platform by late 1918. The device was so successful that the Zeppelin threat rapidly disappeared and the cruisers found their aircraft more and more useful in the reconnaissance role.

The first flight from a ship had, by a coincidence, also taken place off the forecastle of a light cruiser. On 14 November 1910 Eugene B Ely took off from the forecastle of the American scout cruiser USS *Birmingham* in Chesapeake Bay. Ely's epoch-making landing on a ship was also made on a cruiser, the big armoured cruiser *Pennsylvania*, two months later. In October 1915 a prototype catapult was installed on the quarterdeck of the armoured cruiser *North Carolina* and early in 1917 production models were installed in the *Seattle* and *Huntingdon*. They were removed as soon

Far left: The shape of things to come; a Sopwith Pup fighter on a flying-off platform over the forward 6-inch gun of HMAS Sydney in 1918.

Below: The first cruiser to operate an aircraft was the scout USS Birmingham. Eugene Ely's Curtiss Hudson Flier ready for take-off from a specially constructed platform on 14 November 1910.

Above: *Ely's aircraft clears the forecastle of the* Birmingham *while the ship lies at anchor in Hampton Roads. Another tradition was being forged, for the destroyer* Roe *in the background was detailed to act as plane guard.*

Below: *Although this is the platform aboard the stern of the armoured cruiser* Pennsylvania *on which Ely landed on 18 January 1911, the photograph actually shows him taking off shortly afterwards.*

as the United States' Navy went to war, on the grounds that they would interfere with gunnery.

The old British light cruiser *Hermes* also played an important role in developing naval aviation. In 1913 she was refitted with a flying-off platform over her forecastle and another platform aft for stowing seaplanes. Experiments with seaplanes for scouting during the 1913 Annual Manoeuvres proved successful but the old cruiser was stripped and laid up, only to be hurriedly refitted when war broke out. She was used to ferry aircraft across the English Channel to the flying base set up at Dunkirk but on 31 October 1914 she was torpedoed by a U-Boat.

Other countries favoured cruisers for conversion to aircraft carriers. In 1911-12 the old French hybrid cruiser/torpedo depot ship *Foudre* was converted to a 'floatplane' mother ship, with a hangar amidships. Later in 1912 her aircraft handling was improved by the addition of another hangar and a flying-off platform, which allowed her to launch a Caudron G.III in May 1914 for the first time. During the war she served in the Levant, helping to blockade the coast of Syria and to patrol the Aegean.

The German Navy reduced most of its armoured cruisers to reserve in 1915-16 to ease the desperate shortage of manpower, but in 1917 plans were drawn up to convert the old *Roon* (launched in 1903) to operate seaplanes. This involved cutting her down by a deck aft and

replacing the twin 8.3-inch gun turret with two hangars. After nearly two years of planning the project was dropped but a similar conversion was provided for the light cruiser *Stuttgart* in only three months. She completed her refit in May 1918 and could operate three floatplanes.

As already mentioned, the Royal Navy made a minimum of alteration to its standard light cruiser design, and

from the *Caroline* Class developed a series of 'stretched' variants. There were other cruisers built to meet real or imagined wartime requirements. The most unusual of these were three 'large light cruisers' or small battlecruisers ordered by Lord Fisher in 1915. If the original battlecruisers were not all they were claimed to be, these can only be described as grotesque aberrations. The *Glorious* and *Courageous*, both with

Above: *The successful Eugene Ely, having landed on the* Pennsylvania *safely, prepares to take off once more to fly back to Selfridge Field, San Francisco.*

Top: *The next step was the launching of a flying boat from a catapult on the stern of the armoured cruiser* North Carolina *on 5 November 1915.*

18,000-ton hulls, were given four 15-inch guns in two turrets, a speed of 31 knots and the same scale of armouring as the *Arethusa*. A third vessel of this type, HMS *Furious*, was to have two single 18-inch guns, and Fisher hoped to use them in support of his cherished 'Baltic Plan' to land troops on the German coast. In theory their shallow draught would allow them to operate in the Baltic and to support the land forces with their heavy guns. Quite apart from the risk of running into minefields, the idea of wasting such expensive and fast ships on shore bombardment should never have been entertained for a moment, while the risk of action against capital ships could not be contemplated.

The *Furious* was never completed in her planned state, being appropriated for conversion into the Royal Navy's first proper aircraft carrier, but the *Courageous* and *Glorious* joined the Fleet at the end of 1916. With the loss of three battlecruisers still very fresh in everyone's mind they were regarded as a dangerous liability when operating with

the battlefleet. The *Courageous* served for a while as a minelayer and when a raid into the Heligoland Bight was planned in late 1917 they were both chosen to stiffen the light cruisers and destroyers.

The British force comprised the 1st Cruiser Squadron (*Courageous* and *Glorious*), 6th Light Cruiser Squadron (*Cardiff*, and three other light cruisers), 1st Light Cruiser Squadron (*Caledon* and three more light cruisers) with four battlecruisers of the 1st Battle Cruiser Squadron in support. The intention was to attack the German minesweeping forces which were keeping channels clear for U-Boats returning from their patrols. As the sweepers were working quite far out (as much as 150 miles from their base), with a battle squadron in support, the British hoped to repeat their success of August 1914, rolling up the patrol line and inflicting casualties on the supporting forces if they tried to intervene.

The battlecruisers and light cruisers left Rosyth on the afternoon of 16

Above: *The torpedo cruiser* Foudre *was built in 1892–97 to hoist out small torpedo boats by overhead gantries but in 1912–13 she was converted to operate seaplanes. Note the hangar abaft the three funnels and the derricks for lifting aircraft in and out. Plans to give her flying platforms forward and aft were abandoned in August 1914 but she performed useful service in the Mediterranean until 1918.*

Right: *Small cruisers like HMS* Caledon *were fitted with rotating platforms amidships, an improved version of the forecastle platform in earlier ships.*

57

November and were in sight of the German minesweepers by 0730 next morning. The four light cruisers under Rear-Admiral von Reuter laid heavy smokescreens while he ordered his forces to fall back but the British ships pressed on through the smokescreens, firing at 10-15,000 yards at indistinct targets and hoping that the Germans would lead them through the swept channels in the minefields. Von Reuter was hoping to lure the British into a trap, between the light cruisers and the battleships. When they finally appeared, both sides were disappointed because at about 0950 the two dreadnought battleships *Kaiser* and *Kaiserin* came into action on an unexpected bearing, firing at extreme range.

Rear-Admiral Alexander Sinclair, flying his flag in the *Cardiff*, ordered his ships to turn about and retire with covering fire from the battlecruiser *Repulse*. As an action it was a disappointment to the British, who had missed their last opportunity of bringing any major German warships to battle. Despite the heavy fire both sides' light cruisers came off lightly; the British ships were straddled repeatedly but suffered only seven hits while the Germans took five hits. The worst damage was suffered by the *Königsberg*, whose funnels were penetrated by a 15-inch shell from HMS *Repulse* which exploded over a boiler-room and caused considerable damage. For the British there had been problems of visibility, added to the dangers of the very large minefields in the Heligoland Bight, which reduced the freedom of movement. What the action demon-

Above: *A few of the British 'C' and 'D' Classes had a combined bridge and hangar fitted to solve the problem of protecting the aircraft from weather damage. It was not a success and was later removed.*

Right: *The old protected cruiser* San Francisco *was converted to a minelayer in 1908–11, and played a big part in laying the Northern Barrage in 1918. This August 1916 view shows the single chute for the mines cut in her stern.*

Below: *The armoured cruiser* Milwaukee *was trying to help the stranded submarine* H.3 *off Eureka, California, but ran aground herself on 13 January 1917. She proved to be beyond recovery and finally broke in two in a gale in November 1918.*

strated, quite incidentally, was the uselessness of Fisher's 'large light cruisers' for in the stern-chase their forward 15-inch guns firing relatively slowly could never hope to get ranging salvoes to group around a fast-moving cruiser. Their only asset was their high speed but this was wasted as they were limited to 25 knots during the action so as to allow the light cruisers to keep up with them.

Another class of cruisers started in 1916 was known as the 'Improved *Birmingham*' type, as testimony to the value of the 'Town' Class. They were called this because they retained the long forecastle deck but in layout they were more like the *Ceres* Class with guns superimposed forward and aft. They were intended to operate on the trade routes to catch the disguised raiders and so were originally designed with mixed coal- and oil-firing boilers. The armament was heavy, seven single 7.5-inch guns, and they were capable of 30 knots. At nearly 10,000 tons they were comfortable, weatherly ships well suited to their task but did not have priority and so were not completed until after the Armistice. They were named after famous Elizabethan seamen, *Cavendish*, *Effingham*, *Frobisher*, *Hawkins* and *Raleigh* but the *Cavendish* was converted to an aircraft carrier in 1918 and renamed *Vindictive* in honour of the old cruiser used as an assault ship at Zeebrugge.

In March 1918, in response to a 'panic' about ultra-fast light cruisers believed to be building in Germany, three more light cruisers were ordered, the *Emerald* Class, with 90-feet more length and 8.5-feet more beam to allow space for double the horsepower of the 'C' and 'D' Classes. Not surprisingly the designed speed was 33 knots, although on a displacement of 7600 tons they were to have the puny armament of seven single 6-inch guns in shields. One was cancelled after the Armistice and the other two were completed in leisurely fashion some years later.

This demand for higher speed was undoubtedly influenced by the German minelaying cruisers *Brummer* and *Bremse*, already mentioned. Although only capable of 28 knots at full load and 30 knots in light condition, British Intelligence credited them with 35–36 knots, and it was felt that the Royal Navy should have cruisers with some chance of catching them. The fact that these two light cruisers successfully accomplished the destruction of a convoy in 1917 lent some point to the British fears.

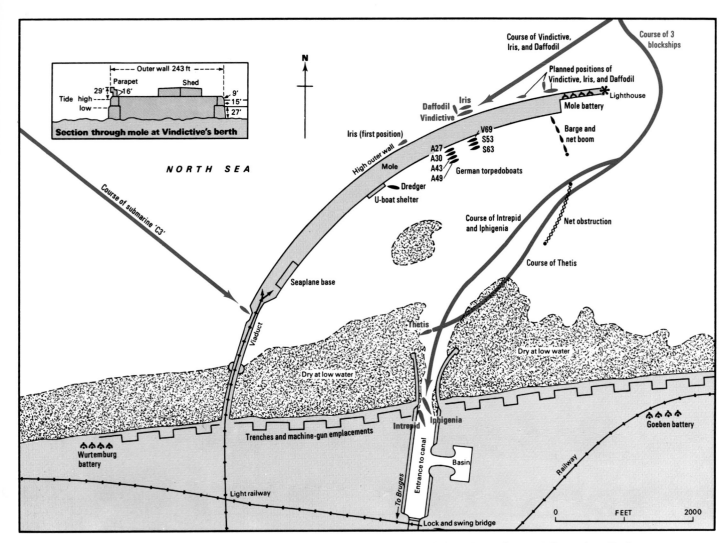

The section through mole at Vindictive's berth:
Outer wall 243 ft
Parapet — Shed
29' — 16' — 9'
Tide high — 15'
low — 27'
Section through mole at Vindictive's berth

NORTH SEA

Course of Vindictive, Iris, and Daffodil
Course of 3 blockships
Planned positions of Vindictive, Iris, and Daffodil
Daffodil — Iris
Vindictive — Mole battery
Lighthouse
Iris (first position)
V69 — S53
S63 — Barge and net boom
High outer wall
Mole
A27 — A30 — A43 — A49 — German torpedoboats
Dredger
U-boat shelter
Course of Intrepid and Iphigenia
Net obstruction
Course of Thetis
Course of submarine 'C3'
Seaplane base
Viaduct
Thetis
Dry at low water
Dry at low water
Trenches and machine-gun emplacements
Intrepid
Iphigenia
Goeben battery
Wurtemburg battery
Entrance to canal
To Bruges
Basin
Railway
Light railway
Lock and swing bridge
0 — FEET — 2000

The attack took place at daylight on the morning of 17 October 1917 and the victims were a dozen merchantmen (two British, one Belgian, one Danish, five Norwegian and three Swedish), escorted by the destroyers *Mary Rose* and *Strongbow* and the armed trawlers *Elsie* and *P Fannon*. The Admiralty had decrypted signals warning of an operation and had given the convoy a distant covering force of five light cruiser squadrons, but they were well to the south, out of visual touch. In the misty half-light the two cruisers, looking very like the British *Arethusa* Class, managed to close to within 4000 yards before being sighted by HMS *Strongbow*. The confusion caused the destroyer to challenge twice but just as she realised her mistake she was shattered by a salvo of 5.9-inch shells from the *Bremse*, now closing to little more than a mile. With her radio destroyed she could not warn her consort astern or the convoy or the distant escorts and was left helpless and sinking.

The *Mary Rose* had been alerted by the flash and sound of gunfire ahead but she too was smothered by accurate salvoes, this time from the *Brummer*, and

was hit almost as soon as she challenged. The destroyer sank quickly, leaving only 10 survivors, and the cruisers returned to finish off the *Strongbow* and the convoy at their leisure. Two hours later 10 of the merchant ships had been sunk and some 40 neutral seamen and 135 British were dead, leaving the cruisers free to make their way back to Germany. As with all such raids there were recriminations, but given the weather and sea conditions two fast cruisers were bound to have the edge over two destroyers. It was a classic example of cruisers used intelligently, and it was to remain uppermost in the minds of the Admirals who planned Hitler's new Navy 15 years later.

Although technically out of date the old armoured cruisers and protected cruisers were found useful work. Many were used as ocean escorts for convoys but several fell victim to mines and torpedoes. In 1918 HMS *Roxburgh* sank a U-Boat by ramming, and HMS *Vindictive* was refitted as the first amphibious assault ship for the raid on Zeebrugge. One great improvement to the old cruisers was to remove the 6-inch guns from the lower casemates, where they

Above: *The raid on Zeebrugge.*

Above right: *Gunnery drill aboard the scout cruiser* Chester *(CL-1) in 1917. She and her sisters were rearmed in 1917–18 with four 5-inch guns and the Salem was re-engined to cure her extravagant coal consumption.*

Above, far right: *The forward 5-inch, 51-calibre gun aboard the* Chester, *with a range finder and a 3-inch 50-calibre gun behind. Although the class was decommissioned in 1921–23 they were not scrapped until 1930.*

Right: *The ex-Frankfurt is near-missed by a 600lb Army Air Force bomb at 1618 hours on 18 July 1921 during the Billy Mitchell trials off Cape Henry. She is already settling by the stern and sank shortly afterwards.*

Table of Losses of Cruisers 1914-18

Royal Navy

Name	Type	Fate
Amphion	LC	Mined 6 August 1914
Pathfinder	LC	Torpedoed 5 September 1914
Pegasus	LC	Sunk by gunfire at Zanzibar 20 September 1914
Aboukir	AC	Torpedoed by *U.9* 22 September 1914
Hogue	AC	Torpedoed by *U.9* 22 September 1914
Cressy	AC	Torpedoed by *U.9* 22 September 1914
Hawke	IC	Torpedoed by *U.9* 16 October 1914
Good Hope	AC	Sunk by gunfire at Coronel 1 November 1914
Monmouth	AC	Sunk by gunfire at Coronel 1 November 1914
Argyll	AC	Wrecked 28 October 1915
Natal	AC	Blown up by magazine explosion 31 December 1915
Arethusa	LC	Mined 11 February 1916
Warrior	AC	Sunk by gunfire at Jutland 31 May 1916
Defence	AC	Blown up by gunfire 31 May 1916

Below: *The* Tenryu *was based on the British* Calliope *and* Caledon *Classes, but with 5.5-inch guns and 25 per cent more power for higher speed.*

Name	Type	Fate
Black Prince	AC	Blown up by gunfire 31 May 1916
Hampshire	AC	Mined 5 June 1916
Falmouth	LC	Torpedoed 19 August 1916
Nottingham	LC	Torpedoed 19 August 1916
Ariadne	ML/IC	Torpedoed 26 July 1917
Drake	AC	Torpedoed 2 October 1917
Brilliant	LC	Scuttled as blockship at Ostend 23 April 1918
Sirius	LC	Scuttled as blockship at Ostend 23 April 1918
Intrepid	LC	Scuttled as blockship at Zeebrugge 23 April 1918
Iphigenia	LC	Scuttled as blockship at Zeebrugge 23 April 1918
Thetis	LC	Scuttled as blockship at Zeebrugge 23 April 1918
Vindictive	LC	Scuttled as blockship at Ostend 10 May 1918
Cochrane	AC	Wrecked 14 November 1918
Cassandra	LC	Mined in Baltic 5 December 1918

French Navy

Name	Type	Fate
Leon Gambetta	AC	Torpedoed by Austrian *U.5* 24 April 1915
Amiral Charner	AC	Torpedoed 8 December 1916
Kleber	AC	Mined off Brest 27 June 1917
Chateaurenault	IC	Torpedoed by *UC.38* 14 December 1917
Dupetit-Thouars	AC	Torpedoed by *U.62* 7 August 1918

Russian Navy

Name	Type	Fate
Pallada	AC	Torpedoed by *U.26* 11 October 1914
Jemtchug	LC	Sunk by *Emden* 28 October 1914
Prut (ex-Turkish *Medjidieh*)	LC	Captured by Germans at Sevastopol 6 May 1918

Right: *The Swedish* Fylgia, *built in 1903–07, was the first light armoured cruiser, with 4-inch side armour.*

were constantly washed out in heavy weather, and resite them on the upper deck where they were far more useful and had good command. The French made similar use of their old cruisers in the Atlantic and Mediterranean, and lost a number of them. The four surviving protected cruisers of the *Grafton* Class were withdrawn from blockade duty after the winter gales of 1914-15 had proved too much for them, but in the spring a new role was found for them. Their elderly 9.2-inch guns were removed and they were equipped with anti-torpedo 'blisters', or bulges underwater, for use as bombarding ships in the Dardanelles. They proved highly successful and both *Grafton* and *Theseus* survived hits from torpedoes.

Another use for the big cruisers was minelaying and a number were converted in 1917-18. The little *Arethusa* Class and the Scouts had previously been used, but only as a temporary measure, with rails and winches bolted on for special missions. The conversions of HMS *Ariadne*, *Amphitrite* and *Euryalus* were permanent conversions, with the after magazines and ammunition hoists removed to make room for mine-decks.

Japanese Navy

Name	Type	Fate
Takachiho	IC	Torpedoed off Tsingtao 18 October 1914
Kasagi	LC	Wrecked in Tsugaru Strait 13 August 1916
Tsukuba	AC	Blown up by magazine explosion 14 January 1917
Otowa	LC	Wrecked 1 August 1917

Italian Navy

Name	Type	Fate
Amalfi	AC	Torpedoed by *UB.14* 7 July 1915
Giuseppe Garibaldi	AC	Torpedoed by Austrian *U.4* 18 July 1915
Partenope	LC/ML	Torpedoed by *UC.67* 23 March 1918
Etruria	LC	Blown up by ammunition explosion 13 August 1918

Right: *The Japanese light cruiser* Sendai, *showing the aircraft catapult aft. She and her sisters were built in 1922-25.*

The preponderance of armoured cruisers torpedoed reflects the fact that their underwater protection had been designed to cope with much weaker torpedoes. However in all cruisers the need for speed made a heavy scale of underwater protection out of the question (see tables on cruiser losses).

The dominance of the British light cruisers over their German counterparts did not go unnoticed in the United States. In 1916, as part of a massive augmentation of the United States Navy, Congress authorised the first of a dozen 'scout cruisers' to work with the battle fleet. These were the first modern light cruisers built in 12 years, and only the second class of this type.

The class which resulted did not materialise until 1923-25 but even if they had been built quickly the design was so unusual as to be quaint. On paper they outclassed all other cruisers, with eight 6-inch guns and a speed of 35 knots, but the armament was disposed in old fashioned double-storeyed casemates on the broadside. Nor was the torpedo armament impressive; at a time when the British were doubling the armament

United States Navy

Name	Type	Fate
Tennessee	AC	Wrecked 29 August 1916
Milwaukee	AC	Wrecked 13 January 1917
San Diego	AC	Mined 19 July 1918

German Navy

Name	Type	Fate
Magdeburg	LC	Wrecked in Baltic 26 August 1914
Mainz	LC	Sunk by gunfire off Heligoland 28 August 1914
Köln	LC	Sunk by gunfire off Heligoland 28 August 1914
Ariadne	LC	Sunk by gunfire off Heligoland 28 August 1914
Hela	LC	Torpedoed by *E.9* 13 September 1914
Emden	LC	Sunk by gunfire 9 November 1914
Yorck	AC	Mined 4 November 1914
Karlsruhe	LC	Blown up by internal explosion 14 November 1914
Friedrich Carl	AC	Mined 17 November 1914
Scharnhorst	AC	Sunk by gunfire at Falkland Islands 8 December 1914
Gneisenau	AC	Sunk by gunfire at Falkland Islands 8 December 1914
Leipzig	LC	Sunk by gunfire at Falkland Islands 8 December 1914
Nürnberg	LC	Sunk by gunfire at Falkland Islands 8 December 1914

of the *Arethusa* Class from four 21-inch tubes to eight and planning to give the 'D' Class four triple 21-inch mountings, the American cruisers had only two twin sets. Before the lead ship *Omaha* was laid down at the end of 1918 the Bureau of Ships bowed to criticism of the design by adding twin 6-inch gun mountings forward and aft and two triple torpedo tubes and by raising the armament to twelve 6-inch guns and ten 21-inch torpedo tubes. However the guns were only in light enclosed splinter-proof shields and the rise of displacement could only be limited to 400 tons by reducing the armour to a small patch at the waterline over the machinery spaces.

Thus at a designed displacement of 7500 tons they were more poorly protected and slower than originally planned. The decision to add two catapults and two floatplanes merely aggravated the problems and eventually half the class had two casemates removed to reduce top-weight.

The most impressive feature of the *Omaha* Class was their speed. With 90,000 shaft hp they all made 33-34 knots on trials but this was achieved at light displacement; at load draught they displaced over 9000 tons, making it impossible to achieve such speeds in service. With their four tall funnels and fine lines they looked elegantly old

fashioned and the US Navy by and large regarded them as oversized and under-gunned.

The *Omaha* design provoked a Japanese reply but as the Japanese were not hamstrung by the need to re-allocate building resources to destroyers they were able to start work on their ships earlier. Only two cruisers had been built during the war, the 3500-ton *Tatsuta* and *Tenryu*, which resembled the British *Cambrian* and *Calliope* types, with four 5.5-inch guns on the centre-line. In 1918-19 five of an expanded type, the *Kuma* Class, were laid down. They had seven 5.5-inch guns and displaced 5500 tons. They and the six very similar

Name	Type	Fate
Blücher	AC	Sunk by gunfire at Dogger Bank 24 January 1915
Dresden	LC	Sunk by gunfire off Juan Fernandez 14 March 1915
Königsberg	LC	Sunk by gunfire in Rufiji River 11 July 1915
Prinz Adalbert	AC	Torpedoed by *E.8* 23 October 1915
Undine	LC	Torpedoed by *E.19* November 1915
Bremen	LC	Mined in Baltic 17 December 1915
Frauenlob	LC	Torpedoed by *Southampton* at Jutland 31 May 1916
Wiesbaden	LC	Sunk by gunfire at Jutland 1 June 1916
Rostock	LC	Torpedoed and scuttled at Jutland 1 June 1916
Elbing	LC	Sunk in collision at Jutland 1 June 1916

Austro-Hungarian Navy

Name	Type	Fate
Zenta	LC	Sunk by gunfire 16 August 1914
Kaiserin Elizabeth	LC	Scuttled at Tsingtao 2 November 1914

Turkish Navy

Name	Type	Fate
Medjidieh	LC	Mined 3 April 1915 and salved by Russians
Midillie (ex-German *Breslau*)	LC	Mined 25 January 1915

Natori Class laid down in 1920-21 had the same installed power as the *Omaha* Class, 90,000 shaft horsepower, but being lighter ships they found it easier to reach their designed speed of 33 knots.

Like the original British 'light armoured cruisers' the *Tatsuta* and *Tenryu* had been intended to be leaders for the new generation of large destroyers building in 1914-15. In contrast the next class was designated as 'scouts' and was intended to displace 7200 tons. News of the US *Omaha* Class forced a change of mind and at the end of 1917 plans to build three of this new type and six improved *Tenryu* type were replaced by a planned eight 5500-tonners. The idea was to match the eight-gunned *Omahas* with seven 5.5-inch guns disposed more sensibly to give a heavier broadside but the Americans' decision to upgun the *Omahas* with twin centre-line guns nullified this advantage. The next step was to be much more ingenious and will be covered in the next chapter.

The experiences of the war, particularly in the North Sea, had done much to restore the cruiser's reputation. However, for a variety of reasons most countries felt unable to embark on new construction while the war continued. Sweden for example toyed with the idea of building three scout cruisers in 1916 but dropped them. Spain, on the other hand, pressed on with a cruiser laid down in 1914 to the British *Birmingham* design, and then followed with two more ordered in 1917.

Appropriately enough, a cruiser played a dramatic role in the very last act of the naval war. When on 21 November 1918 the German High Seas Fleet steamed across the North Sea to surrender to the Allies, it was a small light cruiser HMS *Cardiff* which led the mighty dreadnoughts into the Firth of Forth. It was meant to humiliate the Germans but the gesture inadvertently paid a well-deserved compliment to the enormous burden shouldered by cruisers in the war.

Cruisers and Washington

The cruiser had started the recent war under something of a cloud, in the sense that some naval authorities had questioned its utility. It finished the war with a greatly enhanced reputation, whereas the battlecruiser was now rightly regarded with suspicion. The battleship, moreover, was costly and more vulnerable to torpedoes and mines than had been thought. The growth in size of capital ships had also made them very expensive and after the Armistice many navies looked to cruisers with renewed interest as the most cost-effective fighting ships.

The United States Navy began to plan in 1919 for an entirely new strategy. Hitherto it was the Eastern seaboard that had to be safeguarded against an ill-defined but sincerely felt threat from Great Britain, but from 1919 the expanding Japanese Empire was a much more certain threat in the Pacific. We have already seen that there was some dissatisfaction with the scout cruisers of the *Omaha* Class planned in 1916 and as they were patently unsuited to long-range operations on the other side of the Pacific new designs were needed. This meant much more attention to endurance and gunpower, while it was hoped that the traditional fleet-scouting function could be delegated to aircraft in the future.

The Bureau of Ordnance was investigating a new 8-inch gun and if this were to be adopted it would need a heavier mounting, which in turn dictated a much bigger ship than the 7000-ton *Omaha*s. The argument against this was that the 8-inch guns mounted in the

Comparison of US and British Heavy Cruiser Designs 1919

	Hawkins	*BuC & R Series C*
Displacement (normal):	9750 tons	8100 tons
Guns:	7 7.5-inch/50 cal. (7 × 1) 4 3-inch AA (4 × 1)	7 8-inch/50 cal. (1 × 3, 2 × 2) 4 5-inch/51 cal. (4 × 1)
Torpedo tubes:	6 21-inch (2 × 2, 2 × 1)	6 21-inch (2 × 3)
Horsepower:	65,000	100,000 (approx)
Speed:	30.5 knots	35 knots
Armour:	3-1.5-inch belt	2-inch on 1-inch plating

Below: *The USS* Richmond *working up to 30 knots on builders' trials in May 1923. In many ways these light cruisers lagged behind their contemporaries, emphasising the US Navy's lack of practice in ship design before 1917.*

old armoured cruisers were as slow-firing as battleships' 12-inch guns; the alternative put forward by many officers was to 'smother' an enemy with more rapid salvoes of 6-inch shells. There was some truth in the argument, for a slow-firing 8-inch gun would find it hard to register hits on another cruiser moving fast, unless director-control was provided. It was for this reason that the British had equipped all their modern cruisers for director-firing in 1916–17.

The supporters of 6-inch gun cruisers pointed to the success of the British war-time types and claimed that the deployment of the big *Hawkins* Class with their 7.5-inch guns to foreign stations indicated the Royal Navy's dissatisfaction with them. This was hardly the case, for the *Arethusa* Class and the early 'Cs' were quite unsuited to serve outside the North Sea, whereas the *Hawkins* and her sisters were specifically designed for the trade routes. To resolve these doubts the Bureau of Construction and Repair began work on two parallel series of cruiser designs in 1919: one, Series A, would be an improved *Omaha* with 36 knots on 6850 tons, while Series B ended up as an 8100-tonner armed with two twin 8-inch turrets and capable of 35 knots. These two designs were in response to specific requests from the General Board, but at the same time (February 1919) the Preliminary Design section of BuC&R started work off its own bat on a reply to the British *Hawkins* Class (see table opposite).

The main weakness of this and other US designs was the requirement for excessive speed, for it meant unarmoured gun-mountings and at best a meagre scale of protection to the hull. One critic at the Office of Operations pointed out that 30 knots was more than ample, although he went on to ask for two

Above: *The dirigible* Los Angeles *and two blimps over the light cruiser* Raleigh *during manoeuvres off Atlantic City in October 1930.*

totally contradictory features, good endurance and seaworthiness on much smaller dimensions. This was to be a recurring theme in discussions on cruisers: high speed in a seaway and large fuel stowage inevitably meant a bigger and more expensive cruiser, with a big crew and higher operating cost. This was the real British objection to the *Hawkins* class, not their fighting qualities.

The argument ground on and by April 1921 the design had changed to a requirement for eight 8-inch guns, a

radius of action of 10,000 miles and a speed of 34 knots. The armour would be very thin, a 1.5-inch belt and 1–1.5-inch decks. Although alternatives were produced as low as 8250 tons and as high as 12,000 tons there was some attempt to stabilise at 10,000 tons; it must be remembered that this was the sort of tonnage of a pre-war armoured cruiser, and within living memory battleships had displaced little more.

The British were not unduly worried about cruisers, having more than enough to meet current requirements and sufficient experience to know exactly what they wanted. The French, on the other hand, had neglected the light cruiser before 1914 and were very anxious to build some incorporating modern ideas, while the Italians as their closest rivals were virtually bound to follow suit. Early in 1920 plans were drawn up by the French Ministry of Marine for six 5200-ton light cruisers with a speed of 30 knots and armed with eight 5.5-inch (138.6-mm) guns, but in the post-war financial chaos the project was shelved for the moment.

The Japanese were keeping a wary eye on the Americans and as early as 1918 had drafted rough designs for an 8000-ton scout cruiser, armed with five or six twin 5.5-inch gun mountings or four twin 8-inch, and a speed of 35.5 knots. The design was at such an undefined stage that although the Cabinet Council authorised the building of one per year for four years, alongside the existing 5500-ton type, the Naval General Staff and Navy Department asked for them to be deferred. The US General Board's decision late in 1920 to increase the *Omaha*'s armament to 12 guns was one reason and the visit of HMS *Hawkins* to Japan was another. Unlike the Americans, the Japanese were very impressed by the British cruiser, particularly because of her weight of broadside. The 5500-ton *Kuma*'s broadside of six 5.5-inch delivered 228kg of shells against 544kg from the *Hawkins* and even the 12-gun version of the projected scouts would only deliver 456kg.

The upshot was that the Japanese also decided to adopt the 8-inch gun, and they drew up plans for a 7500-ton ship armed with three twin mountings and capable of 35 knots. To allow maximum space for the power needed the designers had to save weight wherever possible and so they adopted the same solution that the British had with the *Arethusa* in

1912; the armour protection worked longitudinally as part of the hull, rather than bolted onto the plating as was customary. A further innovation was to keep the longitudinal strength-members continuous, even if it resulted in an undulating deck-line. This design, the inspiration of Captain Yuzuru Hiraga, head of design in the Navy Technical Department, was adopted by the Naval General Staff in August 1921. At the same time Hiraga was given permission to build a smaller experimental light cruiser incorporating his revolutionary ideas.

Thus the two major Pacific powers had made up their minds to build large cruisers rather than small ones before the growing risk of an international arms race forced President Harding to convene a disarmament conference at Washington. The US President invited the Japanese, British, French and Italians in July 1921 to discuss ways of limiting their naval strength to avoid the sort of costly arms race which had led to war in 1914. The major provisions of the resulting Treaty signed on 6 February 1922 were concerned with battleships, but the American delegation skilfully fought for the right to build the big 8-inch gunned cruisers that they had already planned. To force the British to accept a limit of 10,000 tons they bluffed by suggesting that the four *Hawkins* Class should be scrapped. Not unnaturally the British jibbed at writing off these brand-new powerful ships, but it gave the Americans the chance to claim that the Treaty's cruiser-clauses had only been framed to allow the British to keep their *Hawkins* Class.

The Washington Treaty created two new classes of cruiser, 'heavy' cruisers of no more than 10,000 tons and 8-inch guns, and 'light' cruisers armed with lighter guns. There was discussion of tonnage totals, 450,000 tons for Great Britain, 300,000 tons for the United States and 250,000 tons for Japan, but the

British refused to countenance any reduction of what they saw as a vital weapon for protecting their trade routes. The British had a much bigger merchant fleet than anyone else, but another problem was the arduous war service of the existing cruisers; the Admiralty reminded the British delegation that many cruisers would need replacing some time before the proposed 17-year age limit was reached. Thus, although numbers of heavy cruisers were fixed in the same ratio as capital ships, light cruisers were freed from all restrictions except those on tonnage and gun-calibre. The sheer cost of heavy cruisers would in any case limit their numbers, but what was not foreseen at Washington was that cruisers would tend to rise to the new limit. To complicate matters the British had stipulated a new formula for calculating tonnage; 'standard tonnage differed from the previous 'normal' tonnage by excluding fuel and feed-water for the boilers. Nobody had ever designed cruisers on such a basis before, and not surprisingly the first attempts produced unusual ships.

The Japanese were in the most difficult position of all. Up to 1914 they had been able to draw on British experience to a great extent, and the *Chikuma* and *Tenryu* designs owed a lot to the British 'Town' and *Caledon* Classes. However after the outbreak of war the British became more security-conscious and Japanese constructors were given little insight into the revolution in ship design which took place between 1915 and 1918. After the Armistice, when it became obvious that the United States was hostile to any renewal of the Anglo-Japanese Treaty, the Japanese were faced with the possibility of war with one or both navies, but without full knowledge of their latest developments in technology. It would now be necessary to build in competition with both the United States Navy and the Royal Navy,

but the only way would be to develop their own skills with no outside help. Thus the Japanese embarked on a course, not of slavish copying as so many people still believe, but of daring, at times reckless, innovation.

Late in 1917 approval had been given for an experimental small cruiser to be added to the programme, but work did not start until 1921, when Captain Hiraga's assistant Lieutenant Commander Kikuo Fujimoto was ordered to produce a cruiser displacing only 2890 tons (less than the *Arethusa* Class as designed in 1912) but armed with six 5.5-inch guns, four torpedo tubes and a speed of 35.5 knots. As with the *Arethusa* the expedient of working the armour as part of the structure made it possible to save vital weight, with the result that hull weight was much less than in the preceding *Kuma* Class (see table).

These figures are quoted at length to show the difference which the new standard displacement made to calculating tonnage, but also to show a very important point about Japanese designs. The designed standard tonnage of the new cruiser, first to be named *Ayase* but later given the name *Yubari*, was 2890 tons. This figure was the one which was published, whereas the ship actually displaced 17 per cent more. Puzzled Western naval intelligence departments wrestled with the *Yubari*'s staggering figures and dreamed up ludicrous reasons for the marked discrepancy between

Comparison of Hull Weights

	Experimental Cruiser	*Kuma*
Hull Structure	1276 tons (31.3%)	2510 tons (38.3%)
Armour	349 tons (8.6%)	221 tons (3.4%)
Machinery	1057 tons (25.9%)	1630 tons (24.9%)
Armament	330 tons (8.1%)	444 tons (6.8%)
Fittings and Equipment	375 tons (9.2%)	527 tons (8.1%)
Standard Displacement	3387 tons (83.1%)	5332 tons (81.5%)
Fuel and Lube Oil	642 tons (15.8%)	1140 tons (17.4%)
Reserve Feed Water	46 tons (1.1%)	78 tons (1.1%)
Full load Displacement	4075 tons (100%)	6550 tons (100%)

Top left: *The modern profile of the* Yubari *makes a strong contrast with the slightly antiquated look of the four-funnelled* Jintsu *which preceded her.*

Top: *The* Yubari *on builders' trials, showing why the original short funnel had to be raised.*

Right: *The* Pensacola, *first of the US post-Washington Treaty heavy cruisers.*

Japanese and Western designs of similar size, the most popular one being that the small stature of Japanese sailors permitted the designers to squeeze the internal dimensions. Writing about a later cruiser design, the British Director of Naval Intelligence (DNI) virtually accused the Director of Naval Construction (DNC) of incompetence in not being able to get his own cruiser down to the tonnage of her Japanese equivalent, to which the DNC tartly (and correctly) replied that the DNI's figures for tonnage or weight of armour must be incorrect, for Japanese ship designers were bound by the same laws of physics and hydrodynamics as anyone else. Yet, surprisingly, to this day Japanese warship-designs are often stated to have been achieved on their designed or 'legend' displacement.

This is not to say that the Yubari was not an ingenious design. On her trials she showed no sign of hull weakness and reached 34.8 knots on a displacement of 3309 tons, a loss of only 0.7 knots in spite of being 14 per cent overweight on her designed normal displacement. Although carrying only six guns, they were in two twin mountings and two singles, all centre-line, and so she had the same broadside as the seven-gun Kuma. Another improvement was to give her twin 61cm (24-inch) torpedo tubes instead of the 53cm (21-inch) tubes in earlier cruisers. Although the fearsome oxygen-driven Long Lance torpedo was only beginning its development, the extra volume available gave even the

compressed air Nendo Shiki Model I type greater range and destructive power than any comparable torpedo. The Yubari's torpedoes were capable of running to 10,000 metres at 37 knots, or to 18,000 metres at 27 knots.

Apart from the light construction it was in her machinery that the Yubari showed most ingenuity. As the British had found in 1912 it was necessary to turn to fast-running destroyer machinery to get the sort of speeds required, and the Japanese repeated the plant of the Minekaze Class. But instead of having the destroyer's four boilers and two turbines the cruiser was given eight boilers and three turbines. Fears about oil supplies led to the provision of two mixed coal- and oil-firing boilers, while the other six were oil fired. During construction the two funnels were trunked together with the forward uptake swept back at a sharp angle to keep smoke away from the bridge and fire control, but this was not enough, and shortly after completion it had to be raised six feet. This, combined with a 'swan' bow gave the Yubari a very modern look, and helped to foster that strong impression of unorthodoxy which was to become a Japanese trademark.

Profiting by the experience gained Hiraga and Fujimoto went on to design a much bigger cruiser, capable of matching not only the American Omaha Class but also the British Hawkins Class. The requirements were stiff, with armament

and protection superior to the British cruiser and a maximum speed of 35 knots.

While the delegates at Washington were starting to get to grips with definitions of ship types the Technical Department gave its approval to the sketch design. It was in its way as startling as the Yubari, with six 20cm (7.9-inch) guns, 3-inch side armour and a speed of 34.5 knots, all on a standard displacement of 7100 tons. It was thus well within the limit eventually imposed by the Washington Treaty and the parameters set by the Americans for their 8-inch cruiser designs. It was also possible to start work on detailed design immediately and in fact the order for two ships was placed on 20 June 1922, only four months after the signature of the Treaty. Faced with heavy unemployment in shipyards caused by the cancellation of battleships and battlecruisers prohibited by the

Below: The New Orleans (CA-32) in the late 1930s. She and the rest of the San Francisco Class were the third US Navy Washington Treaty design and in many ways the most successful of their generation.

Above: *The USS* Indianapolis (*CA-35*) *in the 1930s. The raised forecastle reduced wetness and the hangars amidships provided shelter for the floatplanes.*

Far left: *The heavy cruiser Kako as completed in 1926, with short funnels. She and her sister Furutaka had many of the features tried in the Yubari in an effort to get six 8-inch guns on only 7100 tons, but they were also overweight.*

Top: *The Furutaka in June 1939 after reconstruction, with twin 8-inch guns and new bridgework and funnels. She then displaced 9150 tons.*

Treaty, the Navy was forced to go ahead with cruiser construction as fast as possible, even before the Diet voted the necessary funds.

Things did not go smoothly, for in 1923 the Mitsubishi and Kawasaki shipyards were hit by strikes. The first ship was given the name *Kako* after a river in the Hyôgo prefecture and was launched in April 1925; her sister *Furutaka*, named after a mountain in the Hiroshima prefecture, took the water about two months earlier. The *Furutaka*'s trials were delayed by turbine troubles, while the *Kako*'s hull was damaged when a crane collapsed across her.

Unlike the *Yubari*, the new ships had a flush weather deck with an unusual undulating sheerline. Although this complicated construction and added considerably to the cost it did provide maximum longitudinal strength for minimum weight. It allowed, for example, maximum freeboard forward to reduce wetness at high speed, while allowing freeboard to taper away aft to offset topweight. As in the *Yubari* armour was worked in longitudinally, without plating behind it. In spite of all precautions taken in supervising weights the displacement rose by nearly 1000 tons during construction, as a result of what can only be errors in the calculations. The designed standard was 7100 tons, 7500 tons at normal displacement and 8586 tonnes (metric) at 2/3 trial displacement; in practice the *Kako* worked out at 9540 tonnes and her sister at 9544 tonnes in the 2/3 trials condition, an error of more than 11 per cent. Fortunately Captain Hiraga had insisted on a good metacentric height to limit the angle of heel if the ship should be partially flooded. This, combined with the fact that topweight had been

kept down, meant that the ships did not suffer unduly from the increased displacement. On trials both ships were extremely fast, making their designed speed of 34.5 knots with about 105,000 horsepower, but the need to keep down the weight of fuel and the increased displacement meant that the endurance was much lower than the designed 5500 miles at 14.5 knots.

As in the American *Omaha* Class it had not been possible to provide fully enclosed gunhouses for the 20cm guns, and the six guns were in single 'semiturrets', three forward and three aft, in a pyramid disposition with the second gun superfiring over the other two. A very complex ammunition supply was provided, but it proved incapable of maintaining two shots per minute, as against the planned five per minute. It had been hoped to provide twin training torpedo tubes as in the *Yubari*, but it was feared that the high freeboard amidships would cause damage to the torpedoes or make them enter the water at too steep an angle. To avoid this the tubes were mounted a deck lower in fixed positions in the hull.

Because reconnaissance was a major role for the new cruisers, they were designed to operate a floatplane. Work on catapults was not sufficiently advanced in 1922, and so a rotating platform similar to the one designed for the later British 'C' Class cruisers was fitted as an interim measure. However, this one was designed by the German Heinkel firm and was mounted on the roof of No. 4 8-inch gun. Ahead of the gun mounting was a second part of the

platform, mounted on the deck but level with the turret platform. This could be rotated to correspond to the rotation of the gun to allow it to be aligned to port or starboard. It was a cumbersome and dangerous arrangement and was only used for trials for the first three years before being removed.

The first cruisers actually built for the United States Navy after the Washington Treaty make an interesting contrast with the *Furutaka* Class. Like the Japanese designers, the Bureau of Construction and Repair decided against trying to protect the ship against 8-inch shellfire, and opted for a 3-inch side and 1.5-inch deck to protect the vitals against hits from 6-inch shell and destroyers' guns. Assuming that the armour would be proof against penetration beyond 10,000 yards, any heavier scale of armouring would have brought the speed down to 28 knots, an unacceptable penalty for a cruiser by the standards of the day. What finally emerged at the end of 1925 was a ship displacing 9100 tons in standard condition, armed with ten 8-inch guns and capable of a speed of 32.5 knots. In comparison with the Japanese ships the *Salt Lake City* and *Pensacola* traded speed for gunpower and endurance, for they were designed to steam 10,000 miles at 15 knots. Although more conventional than the Japanese ships, they struck an unusual note in having the two triple turrets above the twin turrets. The US Navy had more experience with catapults than the Japanese, and the design allowed for two catapults in the waist, while triple training torpedo tubes were provided at the

Below: *The heavy cruisers* Quincy (CA-39) *and* Tuscaloosa (CA-37) *of the US Navy's Cruiser Division 7 plough through heavy seas near the Straits of Magellan in May 1939, during the Division's voyage around Cape Horn.*

Above: *The* Bartolomeo Colleoni, *one of the original 'Condottieri' type light cruisers. Like their French contemporaries very high speed was preferred to armour.*

Top: *The* Duguay-Trouin *and her sisters were the first major French warships built after World War I. They were armed with four twin 155mm (6.1-inch) gun turrets and averaged 33 knots on trials.*

Centre: *The* Duquesne, *like her sister* Tourville, *was the first French Washington Treaty heavy cruiser. They achieved their 33–34 knots at the expense of virtually no armour protection.*

same level. They also adopted a flush deck with a pronounced sheer forward, but without the undulating deckline of the *Furutaka*.

The British response was quite different. Although wishing to keep size down in order to build the greatest number of cruisers for protection of trade, they refused to scrap the four powerful *Hawkins* Class. As a result they were compelled to accede to the Americans' desire for a limit of 10,000 tons and 8-inch guns. The recent war had confirmed the need for freeboard in rough weather operations, the gunnery experts favoured four twin gun-mountings, and tactical considerations dictated a speed of 33 knots to match the Japanese and American ships. But by July 1923 preliminary calculations by the DNC's department showed that a ship with these characteristics might have as little as 820 tons of armour out of the total 10,000 tons.

Because the gunnery branch would not consider triple turrets and because of the importance of weatherliness, the DNC proposed to abandon side armour altogether, restricting protection to 'boxes' or crowns to the magazines and armoured ammunition hoists, which would afford protection against 8-inch shellfire out to 20,000 yards. However the Admiralty Board subsequently dropped its requirement for 33 knots and this allowed a further 400 tons of armour, which was used in the form of a partial 1–3/8-inch deck and 1-inch internal side plating to protect the machinery. It also proved possible to provide more power on the same weight and so speed finally dropped to 31.5 knots, a small sacrifice for the extra protection.

Seven ships were laid down in 1924-25, including two for the Royal Australian Navy. The five British ships were given county names in honour of the old *Kent* Class of 1901, while the Australian ships were named HMAS *Australia* and HMAS *Canberra*. When the first ship, HMS *Berwick* appeared at the end of 1927 she was not greeted with any enthusiasm. Her high freeboard and

Table of Cruisers Afloat in 1927

Great Britain:

Heavy cruisers – *Kent[1], Berwick, Cornwall, Cumberland, Suffolk[1], Effingham, Frobisher, Hawkins, Vindictive*

Light cruisers – *Emerald, Enterprise, Despatch, Delhi, Durban, Dragon, Danae, Dauntless, Dunedin, Diomede, Carlisle, Cairo, Calcutta, Capetown, Colombo, Cardiff, Ceres, Coventry, Curacoa, Curlew, Caledon, Calypso, Caradoc, Centaur, Concord, Cambrian, Canterbury, Constance, Castor, Calliope, Champion, Carysfort[2], Cleopatra[2], Comus[2], Birmingham, Lowestoft, Yarmouth[2], Dartmouth[2]*

[1] Completing   [2] For disposal

Argentina:

Heavy cruisers – *Almirante Brown[1], Vienticinco de Mayo[1]*
Old Armoured cruisers – *General Belgrano, Gen. San Martin, Garibaldi, Pueyrredon*

Old protected cruiser – *Buenos Aires*

[1] Building

Australia:

Heavy cruisers – *Australia[1], Canberra[1]*
Light cruisers – *Sydney, Melbourne, Brisbane, Adelaide*

[1] Completing

Brazil:

Old protected cruisers – *Bahia, Rio Grande do Sul, Barroso*

Chile:

Old Armoured cruisers – *Esmeralda, General O'Higgins*
Old protected cruisers – *Chacubuco, Ministro Zenteno, Blanco Encalada*

China:

Old protected cruisers – *Ying Swei, Chao Ho Hai Yung, Hai Chou, Hai Chen, Hai Chi*

France:

Heavy cruisers – *Duquesne[1], Tourville[1]*
Light cruisers – *Duguay Trouin, Lamotte-Picquet, Primauguet, Metz (ex-Königsberg)[2], Strasbourg (ex-Regensburg)[2], Thionville (ex-Novara)[2], Mulhouse (ex-Stralsund)[2]*

Old armoured cruisers –

Germany:

Light cruisers –
Old protected cruisers –

Greece:

Old armoured cruiser –
Old protected cruiser –

Italy:

Heavy cruisers –
Light cruisers –

Old armoured cruisers –

Old protected cruisers –

Japan:

Heavy cruisers –
Light cruisers –

Old armoured cruisers –

Old protected cruisers –

Netherlands:

Light cruisers –
Old protected cruiser –

Peru:

Old protected cruisers –

Edgar Quinet, Waldeck Rousseau,
Ernest Renan, Jules Michelet, Victor Hugo,
Marseillaise, Gueydon
　　　[1] Completing
　　　[2] ex-German and Austrian reparations

Köln[1], *Karlsruhe*[1], *Königsberg*[1], *Emden*
Hamburg, Berlin, Arkona,
Nymphe, Thetis, Amazone, Medusa
　　　[1] Building

Giorgios Averoff
Helle

Trento[1], *Trieste*[1]
Alberico da Barbiano[2], *Alberto di Giussano*[2],
Bartolomeo Colleoni[2], *Giovanni delle Bande*
Nere[2], *Bari (ex-Pillau)*[3], *Ancona*
(ex-Graudenz)[3], *Taranto (ex-Strassburg)*[3],
Brindisi (ex-Heligoland)[3], *Venezia*
(ex-Saida)[3], *Quarto, Nino Bixio, Marsala*
San Giorgio, San Marco, Pisa,
Francesco Ferruccio
Libia, Campania
　　　[1] Completing
　　　[2] Building
　　　[3] ex-German and Austrian reparations

Furutaka, Kako, Kinugasa[1], *Aoba*[1]
Jintsu, Naka, Sendai, Abukama, Isuzu,
Kinu, Nagara, Natori, Yura, Kiso,
Kitakami, Kuma, Oi, Tama, Yubari,
Tatsuta, Tenryu, Hirado, Yahagi, Chikuma
Nisshin, Kasuga, Idzumo, Iwate, Adzuma
Yakumo, Asama
Tone, Tsushima
　　　[1] Completing

Java, Sumatra
Gelderland

Almirante Grau, Coronel Bolognesi

Portugal:

Old armoured cruiser –	*Vasco da Gama*
Old protected cruiser –	*Adamastor*

Soviet Union:

Old protected cruisers –	*Komintern, Aurora*
Light cruisers –	*Profintern*[1]
	Chervona Ukraina, Krasny Kavkaz[2]
	[1] Rebuilt 1920–23　　[2] Building

Spain:

Light cruisers –	*Principe Alfonso, Almirante Cervera,*
	Miguel de Cervantes[1]
	Reina Victoria Eugenia
	Blas de Lezo, Mendez Nuñez
Old protected cruisers –	*Extremadura, Rio de la Plata*
	Princesa de Asturias, Cataluña, Carlos V
	[1] Building

Sweden:

Old armoured cruiser –	*Fylgia*

Turkey:

Old protected cruisers –	*Hamidieh*
	Medjidieh

United States:

Heavy cruisers –	*Salt Lake City*[1], *Pensacola*[1]
Light cruisers –	*Omaha, Milwaukee, Cincinnati, Raleigh,*
	Detroit, Richmond, Concord, Trenton,
	Marblehead, Memphis
Old armoured cruisers –	*Charlotte, Missoula, Seattle*
	Huntingdon, Pueblo, Pittsburgh, Frederick,
	Huron, Charleston, St Louis, Rochester
Old protected cruisers –	*Salem, Birmingham, Chester,*
	Chattanooga, Cleveland, Denver, Des Moines,
	Galveston, Albany, New Orleans, Olympia
	[1] Building

Uruguay:

Old protected cruiser –	*Montevideo*

Yugoslavia:

Old protected cruiser –	*Dalmacija*[1]
	[1] ex-German *Niobe* bought 1926 and rebuilt

Above: *The massive bridgework of the heavy cruiser* Takao, *showing the starboard quadruple 24-inch torpedo tubes trained outboard. The photograph was taken at Yokosuka in 1940 after the ship had been reconstructed and was preparing to become the flagship of the 2nd Fleet.*

Left: *The Pearl Harbor Submarine Base in 1932. In the foreground the* Alton *can be seen, formerly the cruiser* Chicago. *She foundered in 1936 while in tow to San Francisco.*

three funnels seemed more appropriate to an ocean liner, especially when compared with the sleek lines of the *Furutaka*. The lack of visible armour was the chief complaint against them and as the standard tonnage of the *Furutaka* was believed to be only 7100 tons the *Kent* Class seemed poor bargains indeed. Many critics seem to have been unduly prejudiced by the three funnels and high freeboard, for the system of internal protection was as adequate as the thin external plating in the Japanese and American ships and in addition there was good underwater protection in the form of 'bulges'.

The armament of the 'Counties' was impressive, four twin 8-inch mountings capable of elevating up to 70 degrees for use in firing barrages against aircraft. This feature made the mountings very complex and as in addition great attention had been paid to safety interlocks, the mounting gave considerable trouble when it first appeared. However these teething troubles were cured and it is recorded that HMS *Kent* was able to fire one 8-inch shell every 11.6 seconds. The twin turret proved roomy and easy to work compared to the US triple mounting and provided better protection to the crew than the Japanese single 'semi-turret'. The main weakness of the design was its deck armour, which was adequate against gunfire but not against air attack; in that respect the *Salt Lake City* was better, while the *Furutaka* was on a par with the *Kent*.

Below: *The Italian heavy cruiser* Gorizia *running trials in 1931, with no 8-inch gun turrets fitted. Like the Japanese the Italians saw no need to inform foreign navies of the fact that their phenomenal trial speeds were obtained on unrealistic displacements.*

In April 1922 the French Chamber of Deputies voted funds for the first cruisers built in more than 15 years, three 7000-ton light cruisers to remedy the grave deficiency of the Fleet in scouting vessels. The *Duguay Trouin* Class carried four twin 6.1-inch (155mm) gun-mountings and made 33 knots on trials, but at the cost of virtually nothing but splinterproof plating. Two years later funds were voted for two heavy cruisers, the first to be built to conform to the Washington Treaty limitations. The *Duquesne* and *Tourville* were little more than 8-inch gunned versions of the light cruisers, with only 430 tons of armour so as to allow a speed of 33.75 knots. Endurance was lower than the Japanese cruisers, 4500 miles at 15 knots, sufficient for the Mediterranean but not enough for operations on the trade routes.

It was left to the Italians to complete the Washington cycle. In 1925 two heavy cruisers were begun, to be named *Trento* and *Trieste*. In keeping with a standing policy of building fast ships they were designed for 35 knots, but once more armour was hardly adequate, a shallow waterline belt and a partial deck. To make matters worse the Italian Navy had developed the bad habit of running trials under unrealistic conditions, without ammunition and in some cases without gun mountings installed. This was partly a result of adhering to the old contractual basis of accepting the bare hull from the builders and then handing her over to the armament suppliers, but it meant that the actual sea speed in full load condition was much lower. Thus the *Trento* made 35.6 knots on an eight-hour trial with nearly 147,000 horsepower, but could count on only 30 knots when fully loaded.

It is surprising to see from this list (pp. 76–77) that many old armoured cruisers still remained active. The French and Italians used their veterans mainly for training and in some cases they were not actually seagoing. The United States Navy, on the other hand, was very short of ships suitable for duty as flagships and retained the old cruisers until sufficient new heavy cruisers were built. Like the Japanese they were busily engaged in modernising and rebuilding their older battleships and made up numbers with these imposing old ships. Their heavy demands on manpower made them an expensive luxury and the majority of them would disappear within four or five years.

The dreadnought SMS Thuringen *pours 11-inch broadsides into the British armoured cruiser* Black Prince *(right), which had inadvertently blundered into the German battle fleet during the night action at Jutland.*

Above: *'Like a minnow leading a shoal of whales', the light cruiser HMS* Cardiff *leading the dreadnoughts of the High Seas Fleet into the Firth of Forth in November 1918.*

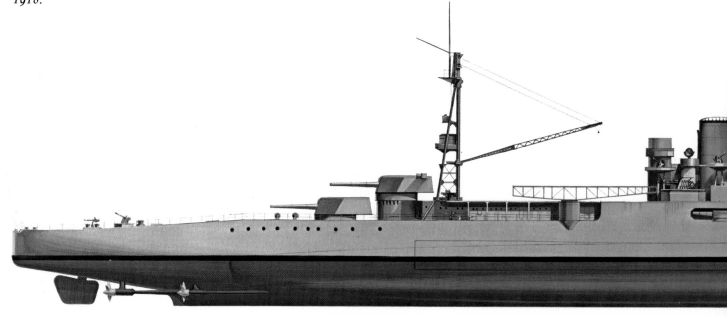

Below: *The Japanese heavy cruiser
Takao displaced 13,610 tons in standard
condition and mounted ten 8-inch guns in
twin turrets, four 4.7-inch AA and eight
24-inch torpedo tubes. By 1944 she had
sixty 25mm AA guns as well as twin
5-inch in place of the original AA guns.*

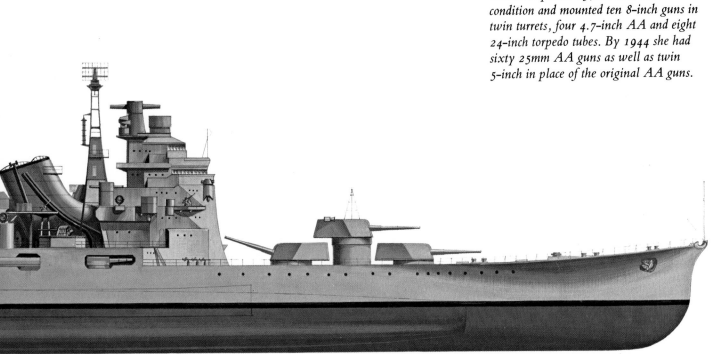

Left: *The heavy cruiser Quincy (CA-39) on 4 August 1942, five days before she was lost in the Battle of Savo Island.*

Below: *USS Minneapolis (CA-36) leaving Pearl Harbor on 11 April 1943 after repairs. She lost her bow in the night action off Tassafaronga in the Solomons but went through the rest of World War II without serious damage.*

Right: *A* San Francisco *Class heavy cruiser alongside a repair ship in the Pacific. The US Navy was able to extemporise bases in remote anchorages, and these proved capable of patching up damaged ships sufficiently to get them home for full repairs, and doing routine maintenance.*

Transports begin to unload at Orote Point, Guam as a cruiser and destroyers stand by to provide covering fire.

The light cruiser St Louis (CL-49) on 21 July 1944 bombarding shore targets on Guam. Note the camouflage and the cordite smoke from her port side 5-inch guns.

The French light cruiser Gloire in a unique 'zebra' camouflage scheme, as she appeared in 1943 after being refitted in the United States. She and her surviving sisters rejoined the Allies after the German attack on Toulon.

Left: *Destroyer sailors watch the St Louis steam out of Tulagi Harbor in the Solomons.*

Below: *Disaster at Algiers, 16 June 1943. After a German air attack two Liberty ships are on fire, behind the light cruiser USS Savannah.*

Above: *The veteran light cruiser* Boise *(CL-47) returns from the Pacific to New York to take part in Navy Day, 20 October 1945. In 1951 she was sold to Argentina as the* Nueve de Julio.

Key to HMS *Manchester*

1 Depth charges
2 Officers' accommodation
3 20mm Oerlikon AA gun
4 After capstan
5 Cordite gallery
    6 'Y' 6-inch gun turret
    7 Cordite lobby
    8 'X' 6-inch gun turret

9 20mm Oerlikon AA gun
10 After Director Control Tower for main armament
11 After High-Angle/Low-Angle Director Mk IV
12 Galley funnel
13 Receiving antenna for Type 279 air-warning radar
14 44-inch searchlights (Port and Starboard)
15 20mm Oerlikon AA guns (Port and Starboard)

16 Twin 4-inch HA/LA guns (two Port and Starboard)
17 Radio aerials
18 After engine room ventilator
19 Cranes for handling aircraft and boats (Port and Starboard)

20 Port quadruple 2-pounder pom pom Mk VII
20A Port aircraft hangar
21 Forward engine room ventilator
22 Transmitting aerial for Type 279 air-warning radar
23 Surface lookout position
24 Aerials for Type 284 fire control radar for main armament
25 'Lantern' enclosing antenna for Type 273 surface warning radar
26 Office for Type 273 radar
27 Forward Director Control Tower for main armament
28 Signal deck
29 Compass platform or upper bridge
30 Wind deflectors
31 Starboard HA/LA Director Mk IV
32 Lower bridge
33 Single 40mm Bofors AA gun Mk III
34 'B' 6-inch gun turret
35 'A' 6-inch gun turret
36 Forward capstan
37 20mm Oerlikon AA guns (Port and Starboard)

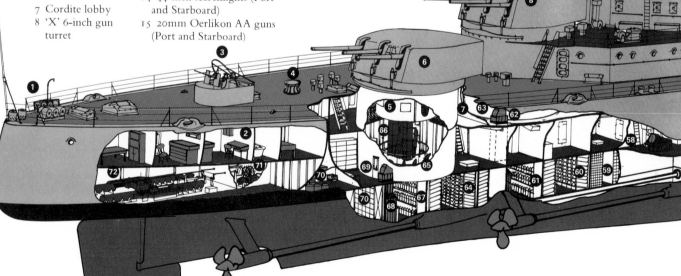
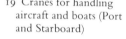

Above: *This cutaway drawn from Admiralty plans shows the light cruiser HMS* Manchester *at the time of her sinking in August 1942. Along with the Southampton, she was the first cruiser to have integral hangars to protect spotter and reconnaissance floatplanes. Note the athwartship catapult, which permitted the launching of aircraft on either side, and the tripod masts which eliminated shrouds and left arcs clear for the anti-aircraft guns. (Drawn by John A. Roberts).*

Right: *The Georges Leygues as she appeared in 1945 after being refitted in the United States, with a new tripod mainmast. The radar sets are British as she was operating with the Royal Navy.*

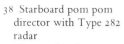

38 Starboard pom pom director with Type 282 radar
39 Forward boiler room ventilator
40 Supermarine Walrus amphibian aircraft, folded in starboard hangar
41 Side armour, 4.5 inches thick
42 Wash places
43 Auxiliary boiler

44 Forward boiler room, with two boilers abreast
45 Engineers' machine and fitting shops
46 Starboard 27ft whaler

47 Forward engine room, with starboard turbine
48 Diesel generator compartment
49 Triple 21-inch torpedo tubes (Port and Starboard)
50 Double bottom
51 Wash places
52 Oil fuel tank (fuel also stowed abreast of machinery, in double bottoms and in hold forward and aft)
53 Starboard outer shaft passage
54 After boiler room, with two boilers fore and aft
55 Shelter for 4-inch gun crews
56 After engine room, with starboard turbine

57 Boat stowage between 4-inch guns
58 After high-angle control position
59 4-inch magazines
60 'X' 6-inch magazine
61 'X' 6-inch shell room
62 Fixed 6-inch shell hoist
63 Shell lobby
64 'Y' 6-inch magazine
65 Loading platform
66 Revolving 6-inch shell hoist
67 'Y' 6-inch shell room
68 Fixed 6-inch shell hoist
69 Shell lobby
70 Stores
71 After emergency steering position
72 Steering gear

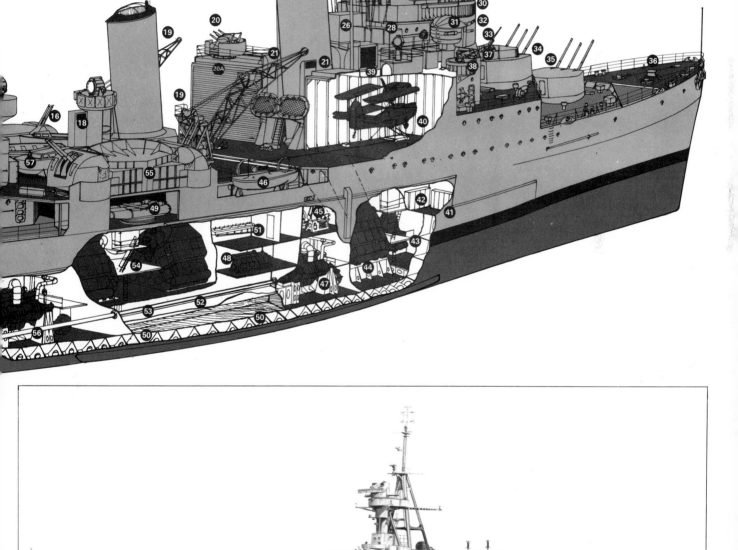

Two views of the British veteran of the Battle of North Cape, HMS Belfast. She now lies in the Pool of London as a museum ship.

Between the Wars

Nobody was satisfied with the first generation of heavy cruisers produced after the Washington Treaty. All were a disappointment to their designers in one way or another, either too big and costly or much heavier than intended. It was hardly surprising, therefore, to see a second series of improved versions appearing very soon afterwards.

The Japanese followed the *Furutaka* Class with two very similar ships, the *Aoba* and *Kinugasa*, but were able to incorporate several improvements. A more logical disposition of guns was possible with three twin 8-inch turrets instead of the six singles, while the anti-aircraft armament was increased by substituting 4.7-inch for 3-inch guns. The hull form and machinery remained the same and as the standard displacement rose by only 200 tons they had no difficulty in reaching a speed of 34 knots. Even so, they had the same faults as the earlier ships, being cramped, wet and lightly armoured.

The US Navy did not like the *Salt Lake City* Class, regarding them as deficient in seaworthiness and over-gunned at the expense of protection. The next ships, the six *Northamptons* were given a raised forecastle to improve sea-keeping and had a more rational arrangement of guns. Three triple turrets saved considerable weight and reduced the area to be protected, but the weight saved was used to provide hangars amidships for the floatplanes. The US Navy was the first to appreciate the vulnerability of aircraft to salt spray and wave damage and other navies eventually followed its example. Two modified versions followed, the *Indianapolis* and *Portland*. Topweight was reduced by lighter masting but the only way to improve the armouring was, paradoxically, to shorten it to cover only the machinery spaces. In the *Salt Lake City* and *Northampton* designs the side armour extended as far as the turrets but only as a shallow extension; this was so shallow that its upper edge was only just above the load waterline, and so contributed very little to the ship's watertight integrity. In the *Indianapolis* Class the side armour was restricted to the machinery spaces but was made thicker, while extra weight saved was allocated to thicker deck and turret armour and to splinterproof plating on the bridge-work.

The British also looked at their *Kent* design, but they were mainly concerned to improve speed and protection and to provide a floatplane and catapult. Not much could be done to the scale of protection but some detailed internal improvements were made. To get nearer to the original staff requirement of 33 knots and to save weight the hull was redesigned without external bulges. A single rotating catapult was mounted

Below: *The* Alberto di Giussano *and her sisters of the 'Condottieri' type were built in 1928-32. Although they reached speeds of 37-42 knots on trials they were very lightly armoured and only reached 30 knots when fully loaded.*

abaft the three funnels but no hangar was provided for the floatplane. In other respects the four *London* Class looked very much the same as the *Kent*s, and were lumped together as the 'County' Class. Four more ships were planned, but they were given a different model of 8-inch turret and further minor improvements to protection. The *Dorsetshire* and *Norfolk* joined the Fleet in 1930 but the *Northumberland* and *Surrey* were suspended in 1928. Detailed plans were drawn up for a totally revised design with two funnels, but the worsening financial position caused by the Wall Street Crash and the Depression led to their cancellation in 1930.

Impressed by the *Furutaka* design and conscious of the need to keep up numbers of cruisers, in 1925 the Admiralty graded the 'Counties' as Class A ships, and called for designs for a smaller Class B type, of 8000 tons and with six 8-inch guns. Only two were finally laid down, the *Exeter* and *York*, and they showed considerable improvements.

Above: *The Italian heavy cruiser* Zara *was a contemporary of the 'Condottieri' Class light cruisers.*

Below: *The* Suffren *belonged to the second group of French Treaty cruisers, but armour was forfeited for speed.*

The shorter hull could be given 3-inch waterline armour, and it was possible to retain the machinery of the 'County' type, giving more speed. There was some reduction in freeboard compared with the 'County' Class but not sufficient to reduce seaworthiness, and with two funnels they differed considerably in appearance. However in spite of achieving all this on a standard displacement of 8390 tons (*Exeter*) the B Class were unfavourably compared with the Japanese ships. It was alleged that the *Furutaka* Class could match them in protection and speed on only 7100 tons, whereas the real tonnage was very close to the British ships, and they carried some 300 tons less fuel.

The *Exeter* and *York* were experimental ships, and differed from one another in many details, particularly in appearance. The *York* retained the tall raked funnels of the *Kent* Class, but had the forward uptakes trunked backwards, while the *Exeter* had shorter upright funnels. The *York* was originally fitted with two catapults, one amidships and one on 'B' turret (which necessitated a high bridge to see over the aircraft and correspondingly tall funnels), but the forward catapult proved too heavy for the turret roof. The *Exeter* was given an

unusual Y-shaped catapult capable of launching the floatplane to port or starboard and because the turret catapult was deleted at an early stage of her design the funnels and bridgework could be kept lower.

The French had intended to build more of the *Duquesne* Class but recast the design of the *Suffren* and *Colbert* to remedy some of the deficiencies. The weight of armour was increased to 951 tons in the *Suffren*, but her sister *Colbert*'s machinery was redesigned to reduce weight and this saving was used to add another 400 tons of armour. Another improvement was to put the armour internally in a sloped belt and to reduce the shell plating by 30mm. Two small coal-fired boilers were provided to increase her range from a miserable 2600 miles to 4600 miles at economical speed, with about 640 tons of coal acting as additional protection to the after boiler-rooms and machinery. Two more cruisers were ordered to this improved design, but once again detailed improvements were made. The last ship, the *Dupleix*, had 1553 tons of armour, as against 951 tons in the *Suffren*. Both she and the *Foch* dropped the coal-fired boilers but retained the outdated feature of the coal protection.

Above: *The heavy cruiser* Chokai *firing her 8-inch guns on exercises in 1933.*

Below: *The* Haguro *in 1936, showing how low freeboard slows a cruiser down.*

The Italians were particularly worried about the weaknesses of their *Trento* Class. It had long been official policy to regard big cruisers as *navi di battaglia*, capable of backing up the battlefleet, and as the four dreadnought battleships were not very heavily protected there was all the more reason for re-inforcing them with powerful cruisers. The Deputy Chief of Staff, Rear-Admiral Romeo Bernotti, recommended the building of 15,000-ton cruisers, but as this was forbidden by international treaty the Naval Staff compromised with a slower but better-armoured version of the *Trento*. She was to have a sea speed of 32 knots, 200mm (7.9-inch) armour and eight 8-inch guns.

Even the most ingenious Italian ship designers could not reconcile such requirements on a standard displacement of 10,000 tons, and it was soon clear that the armour had to be thinned drastically or a pair of 8-inch guns had to be sacrificed. It was decided that six guns would be permissible provided that three ships were built, but when the politicians refused to vote money for more than two cruisers the designers were told to retain eight guns and make sacrifices elsewhere. Even so, as the Staff stipulated 150mm (5.9-inch) armour

amidships the standard displacement worked out at 11,500 tons. This was a serious overrun, and by concealing the fact that the new ships were 15 per cent over the Treaty limit the Italian Navy established a new fashion for outright cheating.

The two cruisers, to be called *Fiume* and *Zara*, were ordered under the 1928-29 Programme and commissioned late in 1931. Another two ships, the *Gorizia* and *Pola* were built in 1930-32 to provide a powerful squadron of four, followed by a third unit of the faster *Trento* type, named *Bolzano*. This ship incorporated many of the features of the *Zara* Class, but had the machinery and light-scale armouring of the *Trento* Class. For a while the four *Zaras* were referred to as armoured cruisers to distinguish them from the 'light' cruisers of the *Trento* and *Alberico da Barbiano* Classes but eventually the Italian Navy reverted to the more usual distinction between 8-inch and 6-inch guns.

Below: *The* Myoko *before her modernisation in 1934-36, during which the six 4.7-inch AA guns were replaced by four twin 5-inch and the hull was widened. She was one of the few Japanese cruisers to survive World War II.*

Below: *This June 1938 view of the Chokai's bridgework shows how the topweight had to be kept down by adopting a pyramidal shape. This resulted in very cramped bridges by comparison with British and American cruisers.*

The Mikuma *in Kagoshima, April 1939, after reconstruction.*

Even with the 15 per cent margin over the Treaty limit it was a remarkable achievement to combine such heavy armour with a good turn of speed. What was even more remarkable was to get 95,000 shaft horsepower (shp) on only two shafts. All four reached their designed speed of 32 knots, *Zara* being the fastest at 35.2 knots on 10,776 tons without gun turrets on board. At something nearer standard displacement they were good for about 33 knots but their sea speed in load condition fell to 29 knots. With 2150 tonnes of oil fuel they had a respectable endurance of over 5000 miles at 16 knots, more than adequate for the Mediterranean.

The Japanese, having astonished the rest of the world, now found themselves outclassed by the new 10,000-ton cruisers. Conforming to their doctrine of building ships equal or superior to all contemporaries they were forced to move up the scale. Captain (later Vice-Admiral) Hiraga expanded the *Kinugasa* design to enable two more twin 8-inch gun-mountings to be incorporated and another inch of side armour. However once again the price had to be paid in excess weight, and the design worked out at 10,940 tons at standard displacement; the 2/3 trial displacement was 12,374 tonnes and there was no margin of stability. The hull was basically similar to that of the *Furutaka*, with the same *Suihei Kanpan* or horizontal deck with its undulating sheerline. The four ships, known as the *Ashigara* Class came into service in 1928-29 and made a great impression. In appearance they were similar to the *Aoba* and *Kinugasa*, with an extra turret abaft the two forward turrets and a superimposed turret aft. Once again a catapult was provided, for two floatplanes this time, but still no hangar.

The Naval Staff liked the *Ashigara* design, but when an improved design

was ordered the constructors were not permitted to make any reduction in fighting qualities to comply with the Washington Treaty. As a result the four *Takao* Class displaced 11,350 tons in standard condition but, like the Italians, the Japanese pretended to the world that their ships were within the 10,000-ton limit. The four *Takao* Class were formidable ships, with a massive bridge housing the fire control directors. Like the British 'Counties' their 8-inch guns elevated to 70 degrees, a feature which, it was hoped, would permit a weaker anti-aircraft battery of four 4.7-inch guns to be mounted. The scale of armouring was generally a repeat of that in the *Ashigara* but 5-inch plating was provided for the magazines. The method of armouring was the same, an inclined internal belt carried down behind the bulge as protection against torpedoes.

The American answer to these eight powerful ships was the *San Francisco* Class. This class was an expansion of the *Northampton* and *Indianapolis* designs, with the forecastle extended further aft to improve seakeeping and the waterline armour extended once again to take in the forward 8-inch turrets. There was no attempt to match the Japanese ships' speed but they were capable of a maximum speed of 32.75 knots and had good endurance. In many ways they were the most balanced of the later 'Washington' cruisers and all seven gave sterling service in World War II.

The signatories to the original Washington Treaty were well aware that they had inadvertently committed themselves to building very costly ships. This had not mattered a great deal while there was a 10-year 'battleship holiday' during which no capital ships could be built, but as the end of the 'holiday' drew nearer there was more willingness to consider ways of restricting the growth of cruisers.

The British were particularly keen to get away from the 10,000-ton 8-inch gunned cruiser and at the London Naval Conference in 1930 they were able to persuade the signatories to sign a new naval arms limitation treaty to divide cruisers into Type A, armed with guns of greater than 6.1-inch calibre (to allow for the French light cruisers) but not exceeding 8-inch, and Type B, with guns of 6.1-inch calibre or less. The London Naval Treaty went further and laid down a 20-year age limit for the replacement of cruisers (16 years for ships laid down before January 1920) as well as tonnage totals for each navy. France and Italy refused to accept any tonnage limitations, a hollow gesture since neither country had either the financial or industrial resources to outbuild Great Britain, the United States and Japan.

The British, true to the spirit of appeasement which dominated their thinking at this time, voluntarily placed even heavier fetters on their own ankles. As the Treaty stood the Royal Navy would have to scrap the four *Hawkins* Class Type A cruisers by 1936 in order to get down to their allotted total of 146,800 tons, even though only two would be over-age. This was reasonable enough, but the British also agreed to limit their replacement of Type B cruisers to 91,000 tons, despite the fact that by 1936 a total of 121,750 tons of light cruisers would be over-age. Thus if the Royal Navy wished to keep its full total of 192,200 tons of light cruiser-tonnage it would have to keep 30,750 tons of over-age ships. Another complication was the fact that the Royal Navy would still be short of another 32,400 tons. The politicians who glibly negotiated away the Royal Navy's position apparently assumed that if 121,750 tons were over-age in 1936 the balance of 70,450 tons must automatically be under-age, whereas in fact there was a total of only 38,050 tons of under-age cruisers. Thus the Royal Navy would have to keep 63,150 tons of small worn out cruisers in service, unlike the Americans and the Japanese who refrained from such selfless (and thankless) gestures.

There was a reason behind this apparently aimless juggling with figures. Serious disagreement had arisen between the United States Navy and the Royal Navy over the number of cruisers, for the US Navy wanted parity in numbers. The Royal Navy had maintained since 1919 that it needed 70 cruisers for the two tasks of fleet reconnaissance and trade protection, whereas the US Navy claimed that 50 would be more than enough. The United States, without a vast Merchant Navy and empire to protect, was unwilling on its comparatively slender budget to build up to the British total, but would not concede any numerical advantage. Therefore the elaborate calculations of tonnage had to be gone through to provide a politically palatable method of getting the British total of cruisers down to 50 by 1936. It was to prove a grave mistake on the part of the British, although there was little they could do in the face of American insistence. The 1930 London Naval Treaty was by and large a failure, unlike the Washington Treaty, but for the Royal Navy it was nearly disastrous.

Up to now the arguments over cruisers affected only the five front-rank navies, with Great Britain, Japan and the United States all very much concerned with what the other two were doing, and France and Italy concerned mainly with watching one another. However almost imperceptibly Germany had edged her way back into the cruiser game, and her efforts were to cause as much disruption and dissent as the Japanese had done.

Under the Treaty of Versailles Germany was permitted to retain eight very elderly protected cruisers, while all the more modern ships had either been scrapped or handed over to the victors as reparations. New construction was

Above: *The German light cruiser* Königsberg *passing through the Kiel Canal. She and her sisters were built in 1925–30 under the terms of the Versailles Treaty, but weight-saving could not overcome the limitations of the permitted tonnage.*

Below: *Although the appearance of* HMS Southampton *was greeted with dismay in 1937 her raked funnels and angular superstructure gave her a purposeful look missing from earlier British cruisers. The tripod masts did away with shrouds, leaving arcs clear for AA guns.*

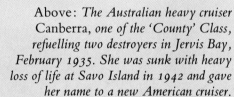

Above: *The Australian heavy cruiser* Canberra, *one of the 'County' Class, refuelling two destroyers in Jervis Bay, February 1935. She was sunk with heavy loss of life at Savo Island in 1942 and gave her name to a new American cruiser.*

permitted to replace these cruisers in due course but they were not to exceed 6000 tons. There was no question of heavy cruisers; the only other large ships permitted were 10,000 ton ships with 11-inch guns, intended to allow replacement of six pre-dreadnought battleships.

Work started almost immediately on the design of a new light cruiser, intended for training and known first simply as *Kreuzer A* but launched as the *Emden*. She showed little improvement over the *Köln* Class built in 1915-18, although some features of a 1916 projected design for a 33 knot scout cruiser were incorporated. When she joined the Fleet in 1925 the old *Niobe* had to be sold to Yugoslavia to comply with the treaty conditions, but the new ship was a great improvement. Originally she had been planned to have four twin 15cm gun-mountings on the centre-line but production of the mounting ran into problems and she was given eight single guns of an older pattern, four winged out amidships and four on the centre-line forward and aft. Speed was a modest 29 knots and armouring was on a light scale but she provided valuable experience after a comparatively long gap in construction.

Under the 1925-26 Programme three more powerful light cruisers were planned, *B*, *C* and *D*. When they entered service in 1929-30 they were named respectively *Königsberg*, *Karlsruhe* and *Köln* and they replaced the *Thetis*, *Medusa* and *Arcona*. The attempt to provide a balanced design on such a limited displacement was not successful; they crammed three triple 15cm mountings and four triple torpedo tubes into the narrow hull, which overloaded it and forced the displacement beyond the permitted limit. Despite having an unusual two-shaft arrangement of steam turbines and 10-cylinder MAN diesels coupled to the same shafts, endurance was only 5200 miles at 19 knots, which made them useless for operating on the high seas. To make matters worse positioning the forward triple turret and bridgework very far forward made them wet. At 6650 tons in standard condition they were 10 per cent overweight, and they were poor bargains in spite of the technical ingenuity of the design. They were unique in having their after 15cm turrets staggered, the aftermost turret to starboard and the superimposed one to port, the idea being to give a greater measure of cover to the forward arcs.

The faults of the *Königsberg* Class were tackled in the next replacement cruiser, *E* alias *Leipzig*. With another 3 feet on the beam she was more weatherly, and the machinery plant was improved by adding a third shaft for the cruising diesels. A feathering propeller was fitted on the centre shaft but when cruising on the 7-cylinder diesels the wing shafts were turned by auxiliary motors. The peculiar arrangement of the after turrets in the *Königsberg* was now seen to be unnecessary, and this time both turrets were sited on the centre-line. In spite of the many improvements, armouring and endurance were still low and actual standard displacement rose to 6710 tons.

In 1929 work started on the first replacement for the old battleships. The signatories of the Versailles Treaty had deliberately framed the clauses to prohibit anything but a coast defence ship. Both they and the framers of the Washington Treaty took pains to exclude anything resembling the old armoured cruiser, fast enough to run away from battleships and powerful enough to sink any light cruiser. Yet this was exactly the category which German designers strove to achieve, with conspicuous success. On a nominal standard displacement of 10,000 tons (actually 11,700 tons as completed) they managed to mount two triple 11-inch (28cm) gun turrets and by adopting for the first time an all-diesel power plant they could provide a staggering 10,000 miles' endurance. Although the speed was only 26 knots and the armour no thicker than the best-protected heavy cruisers, the combination of heavy gunpower, a fair turn of speed and high endurance seemed to be an ideal combination for a commerce-raider. What was more, it was just the sort of ship that everyone had hoped could not be built within the terms of the Washington and Versailles Treaties.

The name chosen for the ship, *Deutschland*, epitomised her importance to the German nation. By evading the restrictions of what was regarded as a vicious attempt to shackle Germany forever, the German Navy had shown that German genius and will could still triumph. Nor were foreigners slow to realise her importance. Dubbed a 'pocket-battleship' by the British press, the *Deutschland* was claimed to be

Below: *The Leipzig corrected the faults of the Königsberg Class by adding 3 feet more beam, and despite having more boilers the uptakes could be trunked into a single funnel. She survived the war in damaged condition.*

capable of destroying any cruiser in the world and fast enough to elude any battleship. It was claimed that the only ships capable of defeating her were the British battlecruisers *Tiger, Hood, Repulse* and *Renown* and the four Japanese *Kongo* Class.

Even if we ignore the 17 per cent discrepancy in her standard tonnage, the *Deutschland* was not what people tried to claim. The Germans, in fact, called her a *panzerschiff*, or armoured ship, and she was no more than an over-gunned and rather slow heavy cruiser. The 11-inch guns gave her an over-whelming advantage in theory but they were of only limited utility in the commerce-raiding role, and 8-inch or 6-inch guns would have been more useful. However she achieved her purpose, and the fact that she commissioned in the same year that Adolf Hitler came to power only re-inforced the message that German sea power had been reborn.

Two more *panzerschiffe* were built, the *Admiral Scheer* and *Admiral Graf Spee* but a further three ships of the type were cancelled. They had served their purpose in bulldozing a way through the restrictions of Versailles and in any case their shortcomings had now become obvious to the German Navy if not to anyone else. The French, for example, accelerated design work on a proposed *croiseur de combat* which had been under consideration since 1926, while the British, Italians and Americans began to plan for 30-knot battleships. The British were particularly worried by the implications of a fast, heavily armed raider on the trade routes, and began to consider what tactics should be used to counter ships of the *Deutschland* type.

The newly renamed *Kriegsmarine* rapidly set about building a new fleet and in 1933 a further light cruiser was authorised, followed by two heavy cruisers the next year. The light cruiser *Nürnberg* was an improvement on the *Leipzig* but the heavy cruisers *Admiral Hipper* and *Blücher* were much more formidable ships. Taking even more liberties with the 10,000 ton limit than any other Navy, they displaced 13,900 tons and so had a reasonable scale of protection and heavy armament; four twin 8-inch guns and a heavy anti-aircraft battery. Unfortunately they failed in the most important area of propulsion. The high pressure steam plant was not reliable and the 6800-mile endurance was not enough for extended operations against enemy shipping.

The French reply to the *panzerschiff* was impressive but expensive. The particulars of the *croiseur de combat* were modified until all resemblance to a cruiser disappeared. A 26,500-ton battle-cruiser emerged instead, armed with two quadruple 13-inch (330mm) gun-mountings, steaming at nearly 30 knots but protected only by 9-inch side armour. Approval to build the first ship was given in April 1932 and she was launched as the *Dunkerque* in 1935. Her sister *Strasbourg* was laid down just over a year later, both ships took over four years to build.

A much more cost-effective solution to the problem was the heavy cruiser *Algérie*, laid down in 1931 and com-pleted three years later. With balance between speed, protection and gun-power she was in most respects the most impressive of all the Treaty cruisers and for a change she was given good endurance, 8700 miles at 15 knots. Fate was to rob her of any chance to prove her potential in battle, but she reflects credit on her designers and was the only European 8-inch cruiser to bear comparison with the designs produced in the United States and Japan.

The Japanese never produced an equivalent to the *Deutschland*. For one thing they had no need for that type of ship and for another their 'conventional' cruisers caused quite enough stir abroad. By 1931, having assembled its full quota

Left: *The 'pocket battleship' Deutschland in Swinemünde in 1937, wearing the recognition bands used by ships during the Spanish Civil War.*

Below: Nürnberg *during her June 1936 visit to Swinemünde. Note her massive funnel platforms carrying searchlights and light flak guns.*

Left: *The massive tower bridge of the French heavy cruiser* Algérie *showing the AA control positions on either side. She is probably starting gunnery exercises.*

Below: *The new light cruiser* Suzuya *running trials at the end of 1935 with two twin 5-inch AA guns omitted. She underwent extensive reconstruction later.*

of 12 heavy cruisers, the Imperial Japanese Navy turned to a new type of powerful light cruiser, well protected and carrying sufficient 6-inch guns to pose a serious threat to most 8-inch cruisers. The *Mogami* Class were designed with five triple 6.1-inch gun turrets disposed as in the *Takao* Class and with a similar scale of protection and speed. This was asking a lot of only 10,000 tons but it was hoped that weight could be saved by the extensive use of light alloy in the superstructure and electric welding. As always the displacement was understated, and as far as the outside world was concerned the new cruisers had a standard displacement of only 8500 tons.

This time the Japanese had overreached themselves, and the first two ships, *Mogami* and *Mikuma*, ran into severe problems when they started their trials in the summer of 1935. During firing trials the welded seams started to open from the shocks transmitted through the hull; electric welding was still at an early stage of development and there was a shortage of good welding rods in Japan. Then difficulties were encountered in training the main gun turrets, and it was found that the weight of the turrets and training machinery was deforming the hull. To cap everything the weight of the heavy anti-aircraft armament (four twin 5-inch guns) contributed to a massive excess of top-weight which made the ships unstable.

The *Mikuma* and *Mogami* terminated their trials and were hurriedly put into reserve at Kure Dockyard while the design was re-examined. By removing the after pair of 5-inch AA guns and the two aircraft catapults it was possible to make a significant reduction in topweight, but it also proved necessary to add external bulges to the hull to improve stability. By the time the alterations were finished the displacement had risen to 11,200 tons and speed was reduced from 37 to 35 knots. The two later sisters, *Kumano* and *Suzuya*, were modified during building to incorporate these ideas and were given only eight boilers instead of 10.

The US Navy was quick to see the advantage of the big light cruiser, for in conditions of bad visibility or in night actions the 6-inch guns could bring a greater volume of fire to bear. It was the old argument for 'smothering' fire as opposed to heavier shells being fired at a slower rate, and without radar to assist long-range gunnery there was considerable validity in it. In January 1935 the first of the *Brooklyn* Class light cruisers was laid down, carrying fifteen 6-inch guns in the same disposition as the *Mogami*. The nine ships built owed something to the *San Francisco* Class in looks but instead of having the catapults and hangars amidships, the flush deck was extended right aft to the stern to allow a big hangar to be built over the square stern. In theory this provided a working area for as many as six aircraft (plus two stowed on the catapult), with a workshop for repair and maintenance, but in practice only four aircraft were embarked. The stern hangar attracted a lot of admiration abroad but it was not a great success. For one thing the stern is the worst place in the ship for recovering an aircraft as the vertical movements are at their greatest; for another the hangar roof risked being smashed in by a following sea. A large resonant chamber so close to the propellers was not desirable either, and any damage from fire or an explosion of the aviation gasoline could cause flooding outside the main protection.

Although the British had fought for a long time to keep down the size of cruisers they too were compelled to build replies to the *Mogami* Class. As we have already seen, the Royal Navy was only permitted to build 91,000 tons of cruisers, and this had resulted in a programme for 14 light cruisers displacing 6500 tons. The cruiser designed to meet this requirement was the *Leander*, originally intended to match the German *Königsberg* Class, and armed with four twin 6-inch mountings but capable of steaming 12,000 miles. Ultimately the design worked out at 7100 tons, which meant that the scheme had to be recast to allow for only nine ships, the balance being taken up with six smaller cruisers displacing only 5250 tons. These were the *Arethusa* Class, in which the Admiralty ruthlessly pruned its requirements in order to get the maximum number of cruisers out of the tonnage allowance. The four turrets of the *Leander* design were reduced to three and the hull was shortened by 50 feet. Protection was slightly thinner but AA armament remained the same, and they also had 12,000 miles endurance. All in all they were a sound answer to a knotty problem, for in the long run numbers of cruisers were more important to the British than individual quality.

The news of the *Mogami* Class upset these calculations, however, and the Admiralty reluctantly decided to build two 9100-ton cruisers with double the armament of the *Arethusa* Class. This meant that the *Leander*s were cut to eight and the *Arethusa*s to four ships. The new design was an enlargement of the later *Leander* Class, with triple 6-inch turrets replacing the twins for the first time, protection scaled up and hangars provided for the catapult floatplanes as in the USS *Brooklyn*. The designers rightly felt that the fifth turret in that ship and the *Mogami* was hardly worth the weight, with its limited arcs of fire, and did not like the hangar at the stern for the reasons already mentioned. The result was that the new *Minotaur* and *Polyphemus*, as they were provisionally named, had integral hangars on either side of the forefunnel and a crossdeck catapult capable of launching on either beam. This arrangement not only saved considerable weight but eased the problems of handling aircraft in rough weather. The two ships were launched with the names *Southampton* and *Newcastle* in 1936.

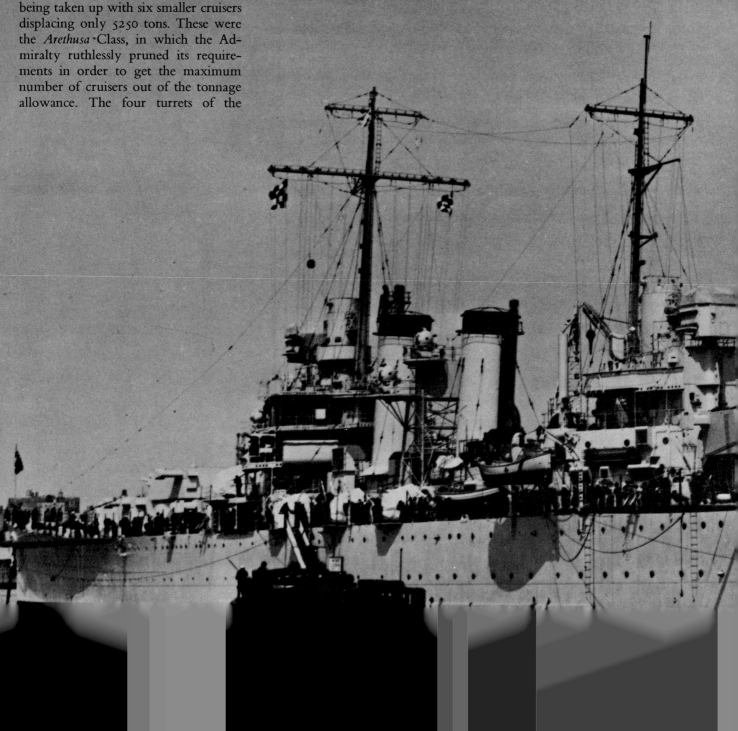

Below: *The broad square-cut stern of the USS Brooklyn conceals a hangar for spotter planes. It was hoped to accommodate as many as six aircraft in the hangar, with two more on the catapults but in practice no more than two were kept in the hangar.*

Above: *The Ajax came close to the ideal cruiser for the Royal Navy, with 12,000 miles' endurance and a good balance of speed and armament on 7000 tons.*

By the mid-1930s the hidden trap in the London Naval Treaty was making itself felt, and the British position was becoming intolerable. In 1935 Great Britain took the bull by the horns and negotiated a naval treaty with Germany, in which the *Kriegsmarine* agreed to limit itself to 35 per cent of the Royal Navy's strength. There was no qualitative ratio, but numbers in each category were limited and any alteration in these categories had to be agreed to by both signatories. This effectively limited Germany to building five heavy (Type A) cruisers and 10 light (Type B) cruisers.

The Washington and London Naval Treaties expired in 1936, and Japan had already given the required two years' notice of her withdrawal from their provisions. The treaty of 1936, confusingly known as the London Naval Treaty as well, was no more constructive than its predecessor. All limitations on numbers were scrapped but the signatories agreed to exchange advance information on their building programmes. No more Type A cruisers were to be built until 1943 and a new limit of 8000 tons was imposed on Type B cruisers. This was intended to kill off the 8-inch cruiser and the oversized

light cruiser but there were 'escalator' clauses to permit the signatories to exceed the limits if any nation was increasing its strength in specific categories. For the British it meant that they could get on with building the cruisers which they needed, rather than worrying about the arithmetic of the tonnage totals. At the end of 1934 they had in fact laid down another two of the *Southampton* type, followed by four in 1935.

The sands were running out fast and it was evident to all but the most starry-eyed pacifist that Europe would be at war within three or four years. The Admiralty ordered two enlarged *Southamptons* in 1936, armoured to withstand 8-inch shellfire. Although nominally still 10,000 tons the *Belfast* and *Edinburgh* had an actual standard displacement of 10,550 tons and were among the most powerful cruisers afloat. The new limit of 8000 tons made it difficult to keep the good characteristics of the *Southampton* Class, but in the 'Colony' or *Fiji* Class ordered in the 1937 Programme the designers met the challenge with conspicuous success. They retained the twelve 6-inch guns and had a more effective distribution of the armour, all for a slight decrease in speed.

There was also the vexing problem of what to do with the old light cruisers left over from the previous war. The 'E' Class was relatively modern and could serve on the trade routes but the *Hawkins* Class was supposed to be scrapped in 1936 to comply with the 1930 Treaty and the smaller 'C' and 'D' Classes were too small to be effectively armed for front-line duties. In 1935 experimental modernisation had been carried out on the *Coventry* and *Curlew*, with their 6-inch guns replaced by single 4-inch anti-aircraft guns and a multiple pom-pom, for use in the Mediterranean as AA escorts. They had proved a great success, and in 1938–39 the *Cairo*, *Calcutta*, *Capetown* and *Carlisle* were in hand for more modern re-armament and the remainder were earmarked for similar conversion as soon as dockyard resources were available. At the same time a new type of light cruiser was under consideration for the big Re-armament Programme which was to begin in 1937 as soon as the Treaty restrictions lapsed.

Left: *The German light cruiser* Köln *served with the Non-intervention Patrol in Spanish waters during the Civil War.*

Below: *The French minelayer* Pluton *was built in 1928–31 but early in 1939 she was refitted as a training ship and renamed* La Tour d'Auvergne. *Shortly after this photograph was taken she blew up after an internal explosion.*

Below: *The Swedish Gotland was the first hybrid carrier/cruiser, with eight Osprey floatplanes catapulted from a flat deck aft and six 6-inch guns in twin and single mountings. However, they still had to be hoisted inboard by crane.*

Below: *The cruiser-minelayer* Emile Bertin *averaged over 36 knots for eight hours on trials, but lacked endurance. She is seen here in 1944 after she had joined the Allies and was refitted in the United States.*

With the success of the *Curlew* and *Coventry* in mind and the growing threat of air attack it was decided from the outset that the new small cruisers should be anti-aircraft ships. The hull and machinery were to be similar to the *Arethusa* Class in order to simplify and speed up construction. The new battleships of the *King George V* were to be armed with a dual-purpose 5.25-inch gun in a twin mounting, and this was the obvious choice for the new anti-aircraft cruisers. They were given five of these mountings, three forward superimposed over one another and another two aft, with close-range pom-poms amidships. As the hull was only 5 feet longer than the *Arethusa*'s, finding space for the extra two turrets was difficult, to say nothing of the extra men need to man them, and so they were somewhat cramped. To make the best use of the space and to avoid excess topweight the designers were forced to use every expedient to save weight, with the happy result that about 150 tons was clipped off the designed 5600 tons' standard displacement.

The new ships were given classical names like the *Arethusa* and *Leander* Class, and became the *Dido* Class. Five were ordered in 1936, two in 1937, three in 1938 and a further six in 1939. Hindsight was to show that the 5.25-inch gun's advantages were largely theoretical, for they were complex and rather clumsy in the AA role. However a lighter AA mounting such as the twin 4.5-inch would have been ruled out as a surface mounting, and by the standards of 1936 it was unthinkable that a 5000-ton warship could put to sea without at least a medium-calibre armament.

To make up numbers for the approaching conflict there was little else the Royal Navy could do but press ahead with refits for the older cruisers as fast as possible. The four *Hawkins* Class were to have been scrapped in 1936 but wisely they were retained under the 'escalator' clause in the second London Naval Treaty, on the grounds that the Royal Navy was falling behind its rivals. To comply with the Treaty the ships were supposed to be re-armed as light cruisers and the *Effingham* underwent rebuilding in 1937-38, during which she received nine of the 6-inch guns removed from the 'C' Class cruisers turned into AA ships. The others, however, were simply disarmed and laid up, with the exception of the *Vindictive*, which continued to serve as a disarmed training ship.

The French, like the British, were anxious to get away from the expensive heavy cruiser, and after the *Algérie* built no more of the type. Instead they turned to fast light cruisers of 6700 tons to match the Italians' speed, and in this proved highly successful. In 1931 the cruiser-minelayer *Emile Bertin* was laid down, with a designed speed of 34 knots and nine 6-inch guns on a displacement of less than 6000 tons. In her primary role of leader to the super-destroyers of the *Fantasque* and *Maillé Bréze* Classes she was a great success, making an average of 36.73 knots for eight hours and nearly 40 knots maximum. This was also ideal as a getaway speed after laying mines, but apart from some flimsy side plating and a thin deck she was unprotected and had little endurance.

The next class was based on the *Emile Bertin* but without her faults. On a standard displacement of 7600 tons the *La Galissonière* Class had the same armament but nearly 20 per cent less power to permit good protection. Even so, they made 32.5 knots easily on trials and in light condition reached 35 knots on trials. They were also extremely handsome ships, with a compact tripod and short funnels, but as with so many French ships their endurance was hardly adequate for worldwide operations, being only 7000 miles.

Looking back on the Washington Treaty and the subsequent international agreements it can be seen how vain were the hopes of statesmen that they could force navies to build only certain types of cruisers. The quick rise to the maximum tonnage and gun calibre permitted is now seen as an obvious result but it

came as a surprise to almost everyone. The prevailing obsession became, as it had at the end of the previous century, one of matching individual cruisers in other navies. Yet experience had always shown, and was to show again very shortly, that matched opponents were unlikely to meet in battle. The antidote to such ships as the *Takao* or the *Deutschland* was to concentrate a number of smaller ships. The attempt to build a counter to the *Mogami* showed just how fallacious such a policy was. In 1939 all four *Mogami*s went into dock for reconstruction and when they emerged the triple 6.1-inch guns had been replaced by twin 8-inch turrets – at a stroke the Japanese had gained four heavy cruisers, and the rationale for the *Brooklyn* and *Southampton* Classes vanished.

On the other hand there can be no doubt that the attention paid to cruiser design in the 1920s and 1930s did much to further research into new ways of weight-saving and better machinery. The resources normally channelled into battleship design were switched to cruisers, with the result that naval architecture made progress in many crucial areas. However it had been an expensive exercise, and much creative effort had been devoted for little result. After nearly two decades most people had finally accepted that smaller cruisers were a better bargain than big ones.

CRUISERS BUILT UNDER INTERNATIONAL TREATY LIMITATIONS 1922-39

British Empire

15 Heavy (Type A)	7 *Kent* Class, 4 *London* Class, 2 *Dorsetshire* Class, *York*, *Exeter*
37 Light (Type B)	5 *Leander* Class, 3 *Amphion* Class, 8 *Southampton* Class, 4 *Arethusa* Class, 2 *Edinburgh* Class, 5 *Fiji* Class, 10 *Dido* Class

France

7 Heavy (Type A)	2 *Duquesne* Class, 4 *Suffren* Class, *Algérie*
15 Light (Type B)	3 *Duguay Trouin* Class, *Pluton*, *Jeanne d'Arc*, *Emile Bertin*, 6 *La Galissonière* Class, 3 *de Grasse* Class

Germany

5 Heavy (Type A)	2 *Hipper* Class, 3 *Prinz Eugen* Class
10 Light (Type B)	*Emden*, 3 *Königsberg* Class, *Leipzig*, *Nürnberg*, 4 'M' Class

Italy

7 Heavy (Type A)	2 *Trento* Class, 4 *Zara* Class, *Bolzano*
24 Light (Type B)	4 *Bande Nere* Class, 2 *Cadorna* Class, 2 *Montecuccoli* Class, 2 *E. Filiberto* Class, 2 *Garibaldi* Class, 12 *Attilio Regolo* Class

Japan

12 Heavy (Type A)	2 *Furutaka* Class, 2 *Aoba* Class, 4 *Ashigara* Class, 4 *Takao* Class
4 Light (Type B)	4 *Mogami* Class (re-armed as Type A 1939)

Spain

2 Heavy (Type A)	2 *Canarias* Class

United States

18 Heavy (Type A)	2 *Salt Lake City* Class, 6 *Northampton* Class, 2 *Indianapolis* Class, 7 *San Francisco* Class, *Wichita*
9 Light (Type B)	7 *Brooklyn* Class, 2 *St Louis* Class

Left: *The Georges Leygues* shows off her attractive lines, particularly the high freeboard forward and the long quarterdeck. The La Galissonière Class *were the most successful of all French cruisers, and the survivors were not scrapped until 1958–59.*

War Clouds

There is a school of history which claims that World War II started long before September 1939. For those who see the struggle as one between Fascism and Democracy the Spanish Civil War was a clear warning that the flimsy peace which had endured since 1918 was crumbling fast.

The Abyssinian Crisis in 1935 had proved to be a false alarm but it had given the British a much-needed rehearsal of their mobilisation procedures. Weaknesses were highlighted and money was wrung from the Treasury to remedy the most dangerous shortages. For Germany the Spanish Civil War provided even more opportunities, for her armed forces saw considerable action which added immeasurably to their prestige and confidence. When on 29 May 1937 the *panzerschiff Deutschland* was hit by bombs from Republican aircraft off the island of Ibiza she was ordered to retaliate by bombarding the town of Almeria with her 11-inch guns. A bigger menace was the covert operations of Italian submarines, for in their enthusiasm to support the Nationalists the Italian submariners did not always identify their targets. The German light cruiser *Leipzig* was attacked by an unknown submarine off Oran in August 1937 and later that month the *Iride* was severely counter-attacked after attacking HMS *Havock*.

The Spanish Navy's cruisers played an important part in the conflict and incidentally demonstrated what is probably the last classic instance of blockade work. When the first revolt started in July 1936 two new heavy cruisers fitting out at El Ferrol were seized by their

officers aided by rebel Army units. The *Canarias* and *Baleares* were very similar to the Royal Navy's *Kent* Class and had been built in Spain with British technical assistance, but were still unfit to go to sea. Although the old battleship *España* and the modern light cruiser *Almirante Cervera* (broadly similar to the British *Emerald* and *Enterprise*) also went over to General Francisco Franco-Bahamonde's Nationalists the bulk of the Fleet, comprising another old battleship, three light cruisers, 15 destroyers and 10 submarines remained in Republican hands. However their effectiveness was weakened by the fact that the Socialist Minister of Marine, Jose Giral, had dismissed the officers for anti-Republican sympathies, and this had in turn incited the sailors to slaughter a great number of them. Like the Navy of revolutionary France in 1793 the Republicans' ideological zeal had virtually thrown away its only trump card at the most crucial moment. Nor could the damage be repaired for the ships were put in charge of lower deck committees.

Strategically the best hope of the Republic was to use its considerable naval forces to stop Franco's forces from crossing from Spanish Morocco to Spain. Conversely Franco's naval commander-in-chief Captain Francisco Moreno had to prevent any blockade from being created. Any delay would allow the ramshackle coalition of Basque and Catalan separatists, socialists, Communists and others to organise an effective resistance which would crush the rebellion.

Moreno's energetic tackling of the problems was matched by Republican timidity; while every effort was made to finish the *Canarias* and get her ready for sea the Republican forces were with-

Above: *The Spanish light cruiser* Principe Alfonso *was built in 1922–25 to a modified version of the British* Emerald *design. Renamed* Libertad *by the Left-wing Loyalist government, she joined Franco's forces and was renamed* Galicia.

Below: *The* Leipzig *was torpedoed by a British submarine in December 1939 after taking part in minelaying operations in the North Sea, but was relegated to training in 1941.*

drawn to Cartagena and Barcelona. As a result it was the Nationalists who won control of the Straits of Gibraltar, when on 29 September 1936 the *Canarias* and *Almirante Cervera* destroyed the Republican destroyer *Almirante Ferrandiz* and crippled the *Gravina*. From their new base at Cadiz the two cruisers were now able to harass the Republicans by bombarding shore positions and intercepting ships bringing war materiel from the Soviet Union. Joined early in 1937 by the *Baleares*, the cruisers blockaded the Republicans with conspicuous ease, and in March intercepted a valuable cargo of arms from the United States and sank one of the two escorts. Although the *Baleares* was torpedoed and blew up in a night action off Cape Palos on 5–6 March 1938, the vigorous handling of the Nationalist forces and the help of their German and Italian allies proved decisive. Despite help from the Soviet Union and considerable sympathy from abroad the Republicans finally gave up the struggle in April 1939.

In the few months left after Munich the British could do little more than try to accelerate their re-armament programme. It had been hoped to build up the Royal and Empire Navies' strength to 100 cruisers but Treasury insistence pruned this target figure to 88 ships. In August 1938 there were only 42 reasonably modern large cruisers and 14 small cruisers, including those 'in the pipeline', excluding the 'C' and 'D' Classes earmarked for conversion to AA escorts.

Above: *The old cruisers* Cairo, Calcutta, Capetown *and* Carlisle *were converted to anti-aircraft cruisers in 1938–39.*

Four more 6-inch gunned *Fiji* Class and three more *Dido* Class AA cruisers had been authorised under the 1938 Programme, but in spite of the rising chorus of public unease the Treasury limits on expenditure ensured that only two of the four cruisers requested in 1939 were authorised. These were cryptically re-

ferred to as 'large' cruisers, which Winston Churchill subsequently referred to as the projected 'Admiral' Class. If constructed they would have been the biggest cruisers yet built, displacing 18,740 tons in standard condition and carrying eight 8-inch guns at a speed of 32-33 knots. Their role would undoubtedly have been to cope with German and Japanese heavy cruisers on the trade routes, and it is an indication that the earlier doubts about the validity of the big cruiser had been thrown aside. However there were other arguments about big cruisers; Churchill later proposed arming new cruisers with spare 9.2-inch guns to give a decisive advantage in range, while the disciples of the 'smothering' theory had plans for enlarged editions of the *Edinburgh* and *Belfast*. This design would have had four *quadruple* 6-inch turrets to provide the necessary weight of fire. However, in the headlong rush to war all such pipe-dreams had to be forgotten, and in the interests of standardisation and speed

only the *Fiji* and *Dido* designs were sanctioned for further orders.

The German Navy, for all its progress since 1933, was not well placed to start a sea war against the Royal Navy. The third heavy cruiser authorised, the *Prinz Eugen*, was not yet ready and her sisters *Lützow* and *Seydlitz* were a long way away from completion. The former was sold to the Soviet Union in 1940, while work on the latter proceeded slowly until 1942, when she began an elaborate

Above: *HMS* Suffolk *on patrol in the Denmark Strait. She was modernised in 1935-37.*

conversion to an aircraft carrier. The light cruisers authorised under the 1938 and 1939 Programmes would have been useful escorts to the heavy units of the battlefleet but they too proceeded slowly and were never completed. To eke out these numbers 11 fast cargo ships were taken up for conversion into armed

The light cruiser Köln *lies at anchor in Kiel, dressed overall for a May 1936 celebration, while the torpedo boat* Seeadler *passes in the foreground.*

Above: *The incomplete heavy cruiser* Lützow *leaving Bremen for Leningrad in 1940, part of Hitler's aid to Stalin. As the* Tallin *she was never completed, but served as a floating battery in the defence of Leningrad, with only three guns mounted.*

Left: *This apparently harmless merchantman is the* hilfskreuzer Komet, *armed with six 5.9-inch guns and six 21-inch torpedo tubes. She also carried mines, a floatplane (visible) and a motor torpedo boat.*

Below: *The 'pocket battleship'* Deutschland *was renamed* Lützow *in 1940 because Hitler disliked the idea of a ship named after Germany being sunk.*

raiders or *hilfskreuzer*. Like their World
War I predecessors they would roam the
sea lanes in disguise to pounce on un-
escorted ships, tying down British
cruisers and disrupting trade.

As the main strategic effort of the
German surface fleet was to be against
British trade it was essential that ships be
sent to sea before any sort of blockade
or patrol line could be formed. On 21
August 1939 the *Admiral Graf Spee* left
Germany for the North Atlantic, followed three days later by her sister
Deutschland, each with a supply ship
carrying fuel oil and provisions. Neither
ship was spotted by the Royal Navy,
although a few days after the outbreak
of war the *Graf Spee* had a lucky escape
from detection when her floatplane
sighted the heavy cruiser *Cumberland*
only 30 miles away. The *panzerschiff* was
able to break away undetected but inevitably news of her presence in the
South Atlantic was revealed when she
began to sink isolated merchant ships.
As soon as the reports were confirmed
the Admiralty and the French Ministry
of Marine set up eight hunting groups.
Six of these included cruisers:

Group F
Berwick and *York* (North America and
West Indies Station)

Group G
Exeter and *Cumberland* (Southeast coast
of America)

Group H
Sussex and *Shropshire* (Cape of Good
Hope)

Group I
Cornwall and *Dorsetshire* with the carrier
Eagle (Ceylon)

Group L
Three French light cruisers, with the
battlecruiser *Dunkerque* and carrier
Béarn (Brest)

Group M
Two French heavy cruisers (Dakar)

Above right: *The track chart of the
Graf Spee's war cruise.*

Right: *The Battle of the River Plate.*

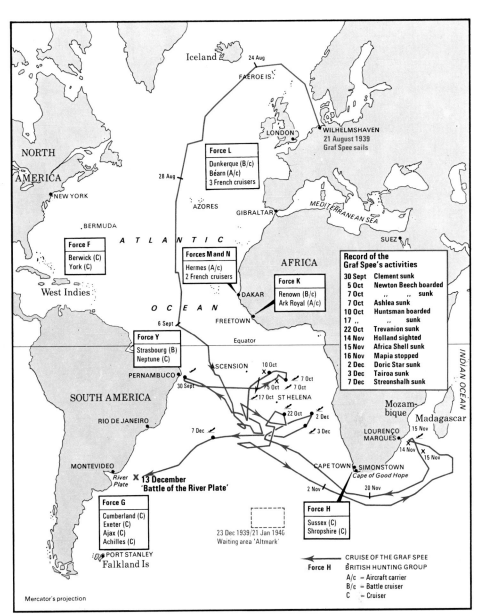

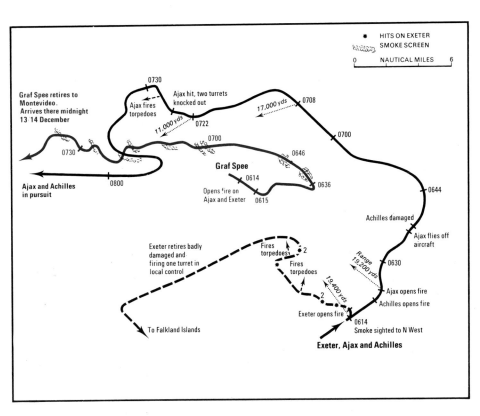

As reports of sinkings continued to come in from the South Atlantic the Admiralty sifted them to try to predict the next move. Force G, under Commodore Henry Harwood RN was reinforced by the light cruiser *Ajax*, and when the *Exeter* had to leave her station for repairs at the Falkland Islands the newly arrived New Zealand *Achilles* (sister ship of HMS *Ajax*) was sent to take her place. As always the temptation was to spread ships around but with so powerful an enemy ship the Admiralty wisely ordered the Commodore to keep his force concentrated, and he chose instead to cover the focal area around the River Plate. He reasoned that the concentration of British shipping carrying beef from Argentina and Uruguay would sooner or later attract a commerce-raider, and so it turned out. At 0608 on the morning of 13 December the *Exeter* sent a report that she had sighted what she thought to be a pocket-battleship.

Although on paper Harwood's three cruisers were at a great disadvantage it was not going to be a one-sided affair. For a start his ships were experienced and in accordance with current Admiralty orders his ships had exercised for such an eventuality, with *Exeter* herself playing the role of attacker only a few months earlier. The principle was to use speed to retain the tactical advantage over the enemy and to disperse the defending cruisers. This had the double advantage of not allowing the enemy's fire the luxury of a single easy target and also permitting each cruiser to spot the others' fall of shot at long range, a process known as 'flank marking'. Unfortunately the 8-inch gunned *Cumberland* had been detached to the Falkland Islands to effect urgent machinery repairs, leaving only the two light cruisers to support the *Exeter*.

The *Exeter* was the first to be fired on and inevitably bore the brunt of the *Graf Spee*'s fire (her lookouts thought at first that they were faced by a cruiser and two destroyers, being misled by the single-funnelled *Ajax* and *Achilles*). The British cruiser was soon heavily hit, a heavy shell wrecked 'B' turret and caused many casualties on the bridge. After an hour only 'Y' turret remained in action, the ship was listing 7-10 degrees to starboard and was 3 feet down by the bows. She might have been in an even worse condition had the *Ajax* and *Achilles* not repeatedly darted into range and then retreated under cover of smoke.

Right: *A Loire-Nieuport 130 floatplane on the after 6-inch triple turret of the cruiser* Gloire. *The French Navy was unusual in preferring flying boats to seaplanes and used the Hein Mat method of recovery.*

Inset: *Gunners at their twin 3.5-inch (90mm) twin AA guns on board the light cruiser* Marseillaise. *The ship was operating off Halifax, Nova Scotia in December 1939, escorting Canadian troop convoys to Great Britain.*

These picador tactics forced the *Graf Spee* to shift target several times to chase the light cruisers off before returning to its main target, the *Exeter*. In all, three 8-inch hits and seventeen 6-inch hits were scored on the German ship, killing 36 men and wounding 59, in return for several hits on the two light cruisers. It is interesting to note that the *Graf Spee*'s gunnery officer later commented wryly that the devastating effect of the 8-inch shells clearly contradicted the belief that a *panzerschiff* could only be fought by a battleship. True, Harwood's three cruisers were badly battered, but the *Graf Spee* was in a bad position, damaged and far from home, with well over half of her ammunition expended.

The *Graf Spee* finally gave up the task of trying to shake off the British cruisers and sought refuge in neutral Uruguayan waters. British diplomatic pressure prevented the Germans from staying more than 72 hours, and every minute increased the risk of more heavy units arriving to bottle her in Montevideo. In fact only the *Cumberland* arrived on the night of 14-15 December but adroit propaganda led the German authorities to believe that the battlecruiser *Renown* and the carrier *Ark Royal* (hunting group K) were only a few hours' steaming away. With shell-holes in her forecastle the *Graf Spee* dared not face the North Atlantic in winter without serious risk of flooding, while the destruction of the fuel and lube oil filtration would probably prove the last straw for her overworked and unreliable diesel motors. With all these problems weighing on his mind Captain Hans Langsdorff decided that the best course of action would be scuttle his ship, a decision supported by Hitler who could not bear the thought of a major German warship being sunk in battle. On the evening of 17 December, therefore, just as the waiting British cruisers cleared for action, the *Graf Spee* stopped just outside territorial waters, sent her crew away to a German steamer and then

erupted in smoke and flame. Within minutes the scuttling charges had wrecked the ship and left her under a pall of oily smoke.

The Battle of the River Plate gave a well-deserved fillip to British morale in the middle of the 'Phoney War' and dispelled forever the myth of the pocket-battleship. Even though the *Deutschland* had slipped through the patrols and returned to Germany safely a month earlier, her haul of two ships totalling less than 7000 tons was meagre. The German Navy recognised their shortcomings as well, and reclassified the two survivors as heavy cruisers in 1940. To add to the sense of pessimism Hitler even insisted on changing *Deutschland*'s name to *Lützow* because her loss would damage German prestige!

The North Atlantic Theatre
As in the previous conflict the Royal Navy was forced to arm liners as armed merchant cruisers (AMC) to make up for the crucial shortage of cruisers. These vulnerable ships suffered many casualties; out of the 56 taken up in 1939-40 no fewer than 15 were sunk by 1942. (See table on opposite page).

The *Rawalpindi* had been launched in 1925 and had a gross tonnage of 16,697 GRT. Her eight 6-inch guns were the same type as mounted in the old 'C' Class and at 8000 yards she had no hope of matching the 11-inch guns of the battlecruiser *Scharnhorst*. This one-sided fight lasted only 14 minutes, during

which the AMC managed to score one minor hit before being sunk. A year later the *Jervis Bay* (14,164 GRT, eight 6-inch guns) was similarly overwhelmed by the 11-inch salvoes of the *Admiral Scheer*, but this time her sacrifice saved the convoy she was escorting. Out of 37 ships in the convoy only five were sunk but, as with the *Rawalpindi*, supporting British warships did not arrive in time to catch the attacker.

In truth the AMC had outlived her usefulness and was better employed as a troopship. The German *hilfskreuzer* met modern requirements more closely, with a low silhouette, good turn of speed and ability to change appearance easily. Although some AMCs continued to operate in the South Atlantic and East Indies as late as 1943 the bulk were withdrawn in 1942 and converted to troopships or amphibious transports. A much more valuable type of auxiliary cruiser took their place, although it was never formally admitted to be anything of the sort. This was the auxiliary anti-aircraft vessel, a freighter of modest speed armed with the latest twin 4-inch anti-aircraft guns and naval fire control. The biggest ships had four twin mountings, two forward and two aft on the centre-line. Some smaller conversions had only three mountings, but provided with proper radar and fire control they had

Rawalpindi	Sunk by *Scharnhorst* 23 November 1939
Carinthia	Torpedoed by U-Boat 7 June 1940
Scotstoun	Torpedoed by U-Boat 13 June 1940
Andania	Torpedoed by U-Boat 16 June 1940
Transylvania	Torpedoed by U-Boat 10 August 1940
Dunvegan Castle	Torpedoed by U-Boat 28 August 1940
Laurentic	Torpedoed by U-Boat 3 November 1940
Patroclus	Torpedoed by U-Boat 4 November 1940
Jervis Bay	Sunk by *Admiral Scheer* 5 November 1940
Forfar	Torpedoed by U-Boat 2 December 1940
Voltaire	Sunk by *hilfskreuzer Thor* 4 April 1941
Comorin	Lost by fire in North Atlantic 6 April 1941
Rajputana	Torpedoed by U-Boat 13 April 1941
Salopian	Torpedoed by U-Boat 13 May 1941
Hector	Scrapped after heavy damaged sustained 5 April 1942

firepower approaching that of the biggest cruisers. Sailing with convoys and invasion fleets they could provide a massive barrage of high-angle fire and their modest speed was no handicap. Although not regarded as AMCs they fulfilled that basic criterion in that they freed proper cruisers from the wasteful and dangerous task of steaming slowly in a formation of ships.

The German cruiser force was small enough in September 1939 but the Norwegian campaign in the Spring of 1940 cut it to the bone. First to go was the new *Blücher*, 13,000 tons and armed with eight 8-inch guns. She was steaming up Oslo Fjord ahead of the *Lützow* (the former *Deutschland*) and the *Emden* in the early hours of 9 April 1940, intent on occupying Oslo. Brazen self-confidence had got the force two-thirds of the way up Oslo Fjord, with fictitious claims about permission from the Norwegian Government, but when it reached the dangerous Drobak Narrows its luck ran out. An elderly force of

Below: *The new heavy cruiser* Blücher *before the outbreak of war.*

reservists manning the obsolescent 11-inch guns on the island fortress of Kaholm stood to their posts and opened fire on the hapless *Blücher* as she entered the Narrows. At short range they could hardly miss, and the first salvo struck home. Just over a minute later the ship was hit by two torpedoes, fired from underwater tubes on Kaholm. The *Blücher* was doomed, her engines stopped and her superstructure caught fire, and although she remained afloat for another two hours she eventually capsized in the channel. Nor had the rest of the force escaped with damage, for the *Lützow*'s forward triple 11-inch turret had been put out of action by a shell from the Kaholm batteries.

On 10 April the light cruisers *Königsberg* and *Karlsruhe* were struck down, the former by British dive bombers while lying off Bergen and the latter by torpedoes from HM Submarine *Truant* off Kristiansand. The *Leipzig* had been badly damaged four months earlier by a British torpedo and the *Admiral Hipper* had been rammed by the British destroyer *Glowworm* on 8 April while heading for Norway. This left the Kriegsmarine with only the *Emden*, *Nürnberg* and *Köln* to support Hitler's 'Sealion' invasion of England after the fall of France. As the other ships had also suffered heavily it is hardly surprising that the Naval Staff shared the prevailing view that *Seelöwe* was never a feasible operation.

The *Admiral Hipper*, after her brush with the *Glowworm* was sent out into the Atlantic at the end of 1940. As with other German warships her machinery was a constant headache, and her maximum speed was soon down to 25 knots. Had the British known this they might have turned it to advantage when on Christmas Eve 1940 the cruisers *Berwick*, *Bonaventure* and *Dunedin* met the *Admiral Hipper*. They were covering a convoy of troop ships bound for North Africa, and although she hit the *Berwick* twice the *Hipper* beat a hasty retreat.

Above: *In 1939 the* Karlsruhe *was refitted, with four feet added to the beam to improve stability. The forefunnel was raised and both were given smoke-deflecting caps. A heavier tripod mast was stepped against the after funnel.*

Left: *The doomed destroyer HMS* Glowworm *slides across the bows of the* Admiral Hipper *on 8 April 1940. Despite hits from the cruiser's 8-inch guns she managed to ram her and inflict serious damage before sinking.*

Above right: *A heavily camouflaged* Admiral Hipper *in her northern Norwegian lair, photographed on 2 July 1942. She operated with the Northern Battle Group until relegated to training in 1944, and was scuttled in May 1945.*

Below: *The* Prinz Eugen *makes a safe landfall in Brest on 1 June 1941 after parting company with the* Bismarck *a week earlier.*

Although the Commander-in-Chief Admiral Raeder wanted decisive results and bold handling there was the constant problem of Hitler's refusal to take the risk of ships being sunk. There was also something else; the German Navy's memories of 1914-18, when another much bigger fleet had avoided action on numerous occasions. Again and again the *Führer* expressed his doubts about the exploits of his cruisers and capital ships, contrasting them unfavourably with the *élan* shown by the Wehrmacht and the Luftwaffe. Although his directives were partly to blame his shrewd instinct told him that the root cause lay deeper.

On 22 May 1941 the heavy cruiser HMS *Suffolk* caught sight of two big ships close to the pack-ice in the Denmark Strait. She and the *Norfolk* had been stationed there for one reason only, to spot the new battleship *Bismarck* and the heavy cruiser *Prinz Eugen* if they should try to break out into the Atlantic from their forward base at Bergen. Although the *Bismarck* fired a couple of

ranging salvoes at the murky shape of the *Norfolk* the two cruisers managed to stay out of trouble, and the German Admiral knew that it was only a matter of time before other British ships tried to make contact. During the next day and the following night the *Suffolk's* radar set continued to trace the German ships.

The two cruisers might have hoped that their risky pursuit was over when the British battlecruiser squadron came up at first light on the morning of 24 May. However, as we know, the flagship *Hood* blew up following a fire caused by one of the *Prinz Eugen's* 8-inch shells. The exact cause of the explosion will never be known, but it is known that the big fire amidships was caused by the cruiser's shells, not the *Bismarck's*, another example of the unforeseen potency of 8-inch gunfire against capital ships.

During the subsequent chase the *Suffolk* and *Norfolk* hung on grimly, but eventually lost contact. The reason was

that the *Bismarck* had already doubled back to create a diversion so that the *Prinz Eugen*, which was running low on fuel, could break away to Brest. To avoid being caught again the cruisers had adopted the tactic of zig-zagging at extreme radar range, catching the 'blip' on one leg, losing it on the next and then returning to catch it once more. This was all very well until the *Bismarck* made an unexpected change of course away from their shadowers; when the *Suffolk* came back on her next 'zig' there was no echo on her radar screen. This was potentially disastrous but fortunately German intelligence greatly over-estimated the range of British radar. As the *Bismarck* was still receiving weak pulses from the *Suffolk*'s radar (they lacked the strength to return to the transmitter/receiver) she assumed that she was still being shadowed. On such mistakes depend the course of history, and a long radio message subsequently sent from the *Bismarck* put the cruisers back on her

track. On the morning of 27 May, only three days after the destruction of HMS *Hood*, the *Norfolk* and *Suffolk* handed over their responsibility to the battleships *King George V* and *Rodney* of the Home Fleet. Yet again a cruiser intervened with considerable effect in a battleship action, for the first decisive hit was scored when HMS *Dorsetshire*'s 8-inch shells knocked out the *Bismarck*'s fire control. She was also the ship

detailed to torpedo the flaming wreck after the two battleships broke off the action to return to base.

The swift retribution meted out to the *Bismarck* marked a turning point in the ocean war. Thereafter German raiders might lurk in Norwegian Fjords and pose a threat to the convoys heading to north-Russian ports but the risk of a disruption of the Atlantic convoy system receded month by month. Early in 1942 the battlecruisers *Scharnhorst* and *Gneisenau* and the *Prinz Eugen* made their audacious daylight run through the English Channel but it was a 'strategic withdrawal' from the Atlantic rather

Scenes aboard the Admiral Hipper:
Above: *Giving orders from a control
station.* Right: *Manhandling 8-inch shells.*
Far right: *Loading 4.1-inch shells.*

than a shift of offensive significance. The
large scale of British aid to Russia,
coupled with Hitler's obsession with the
strategic value of Norway, meant that
cruiser warfare assumed a growing importance in that theatre.

The first few convoys to Murmansk
were not molested, but PQ-13 ran into
trouble on 28 March 1942, when three
large German destroyers attacked the
scattered convoy. The escorting cruiser
HMS *Trinidad* had already done sterling
work for the anti-aircraft defence of the
convoy and now her 6-inch guns
smashed into the German leader *Z26*.
However when she attempted to fire a
torpedo at her victim the intense cold
froze the gyroscope so that the torpedo
circled and plunged into the cruiser's
starboard boiler-room. She did not sink
and managed to limp into Murmansk
three days later. There she was repaired
with a massive metal patch, hoisted into
place by a gang of women labourers,
and she was ready to return home to
England by 13 May. Next day she and
her escorts came under heavy air attack,
during which one bomb blew in the
temporary patch and another set her on
fire forward. Although she was still
steaming at 20 knots, with her steering
intact, the fire gained control and
eventually the *Trinidad* was abandoned.

On 30 April another valuable cruiser
had been lost while attached to a slow

convoy. She was the *Edinburgh*, flagship of Rear-Admiral Bonham-Carter, and she fell victim to a torpedo attack from a U-Boat. While she was zig-zagging at 19 knots *U.456* managed to hit her twice on the starboard side. Next day she was attacked by three German destroyers, and the crippled cruiser and her destroyers began a grim game of hide-and-seek in the snow showers and smoke-screens. Although capable of only 8 knots and forced to steam in circles, the *Edinburgh* was game to the end. When the *Hermann Schoemann* came dashing out of a snowstorm it took only two salvoes from the *Edinburgh*'s single serviceable turret to cripple her. But the *Edinburgh* had been hit by a third torpedo on the port side, and this had nearly broken her in two. Having helped to drive off the enemy and save her convoy she was finally abandoned and sunk by one of her escorts.

The loss of these two cruisers forced a change in convoy tactics. From then on cruisers were kept away from the convoy, close enough to return if a surface attack developed but never close enough to provide the heavy AA defence which was so valuable in breaking up concentrated air attacks. It was to plug this gap that the auxiliary AA vessels were created. Typical conversions were the small motor ships *Pozarica* and *Palomares* (1895 GRT). They were ex-McAndrews Line fruit carriers armed with three twin 4-inch AA mountings, two quadruple pom-poms and a variety of smaller weapons.

The disastrous story of convoy PQ-17 in July 1942 has been told many times, and one cannot avoid drawing a comparison between the actual fate of the scattered ships at the hands of U-Boats and bombers and the theoretical outcome of an attack by the *Tirpitz*, *Admiral Hipper* and *Admiral Scheer*. The commander of the covering cruiser force, Rear-Admiral Hamilton, had four heavy cruisers, the *London*, *Norfolk*, *Tuscaloosa* and *Wichita*. He planned to use them as boldly as Harwood had at the River Plate battle – laying smokescreens to hide the scattering convoy and divide the enemy's fire. Nobody can tell whether such stratagems would have worked against a resolute attack by the Germans, but the history of other cruiser actions shows that the *Kriegsmarine* was rarely able to match such tactics. Nevertheless, only 11 of the original convoy of 30 escaped the U-Boats and bombers and made Russia.

The Battle of the Barents Sea at the end of that year shows what might actually have happened to PQ-17 if the local commanders had been left to work out the defence for themselves. On the morning of 31 December the *Lützow* and *Admiral Hipper* made contact with convoy JW-51B heading past Bear Island for Murmansk. The close escort under Captain Sherbrooke comprised six destroyers and the distant escort under Rear-Admiral Burnett was made up of two 6-inch gunned cruisers, the *Sheffield* and the *Jamaica*. The German commander, Vice-Admiral Kummetz, hoped to bring the *Admiral Hipper* and three destroyers into action on the convoy's port quarter, forcing it to veer away to the southeast – right into the path of the *Lützow* and her destroyers. What in fact happened was that the destroyer HMS *Achates* laid a dense smokescreen while the other destroyers exchanged a desultory fire with the enemy at a range of about five miles. The visibility was poor, with snow squalls and patches of smoke making it necessary to fire by radar. Neither side was shooting well, the British destroyers' violent motion and constant icing up of gun-breeches made it all but impossible to fire steadily, but the much bigger *Admiral Hipper*'s shooting was equally erratic. It took her nearly an hour before she registered on the *Onslow*, causing terrible havoc. However now the *Sheffield* and *Jamaica* were only 12 miles away, closing rapidly and totally undetected by Kummetz. Fortuitously a heavy snowstorm brought a temporary respite to Sherbrooke's destroyers and they escaped further punishment.

Although the obdurate defence of Sherbrooke's destroyers had slowed the progress of the German plans they were working out as desired, for the British were being forced in the direction of the *Lützow*. The same snowstorm which had saved Sherbrooke and the *Onslow* now saved the convoy, for the *Lützow*'s captain, ever mindful of Hitler's instructions to take no risks, stood off to the east while the weather cleared.

Scenes from the Arctic:
Top: *HMS* Trinidad *refuelling a destroyer in foul weather.* Centre: *The US destroyer* Wainwright *refuelling from HMS* Norfolk *during a joint USN/RN convoy operation in 1942.* Left: *The* Nürnberg *blends into her snowy background.*

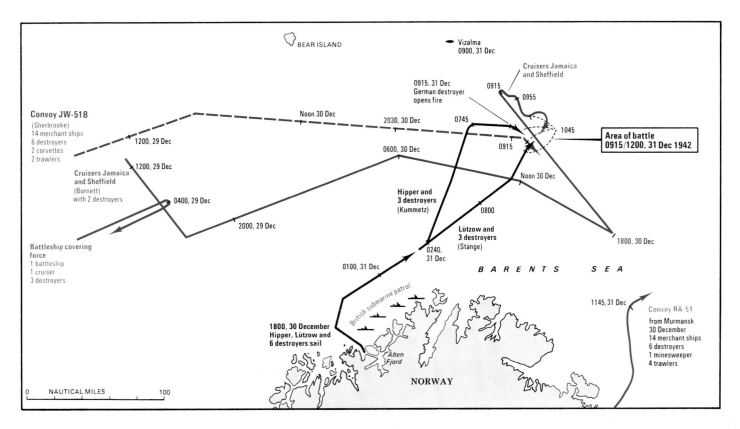

Convoy JW-51B
(Sherbrooke)
14 merchant ships
6 destroyers
2 corvettes
2 trawlers

1200, 29 Dec

Cruisers Jamaica
and Sheffield
(Burnett)
with 2 destroyers

1200, 29 Dec

0400, 29 Dec

Battleship covering
force
1 battleship
1 cruiser
3 destroyers

2000, 29 Dec

Vizalma
0900, 31 Dec

Cruisers Jamaica
and Sheffield

0915

0955

0915, 31 Dec
German destroyer
opens fire

0745

1045

Noon 30 Dec

2030, 30 Dec

0915

**Area of battle
0915/1200, 31 Dec 1942**

0600, 30 Dec

Noon 30 Dec

**Hipper and
3 destroyers**
(Kummetz)

0800

**Lützow and
3 destroyers**
(Stange)

0240,
31 Dec

1800, 30 Dec

BARENTS SEA

0100, 31 Dec

British submarine patrol

1145, 31 Dec

Convoy RA-51
from Murmansk
30 December
14 merchant ships
6 destroyers
1 minesweeper
4 trawlers

**1800, 30 December
Hipper, Lützow and
6 destroyers sail**

Alten
Fjord

NORWAY

0 NAUTICAL MILES 100

Above: *Battle of the Barents Sea.*
Left: *Loading a 6-inch gun aboard HMS*
Orion, *with the turret crew wearing
anti-flash gear. The shell is being rammed
into the breech.*

The *Admiral Hipper* made contact
once more at 1100 but wasted her fire
on the *Achates*, still laying the smokescreen which hid the precious convoy.
She had just shifted fire to another
destroyer when at 1125 a salvo of 6-inch
shells from the *Sheffield* fell around her.
The fourth salvo hit, and the startled
Admiral Hipper hauled around in a
circle to make her escape, but not before
the British cruiser scored another two
hits. Kummetz had strict orders about
action with heavy units and had no
choice but to withdraw to the west at
top speed with the *Sheffield* and *Jamaica*
in hot pursuit. Two luckless German
destroyers, mistaking the British for
their own forces in the gloom, closed to
be greeted with a withering fire. The
Richard Beitzen escaped but the *Friedrich
Eckholdt* was destroyed at point-blank
range.

The *Lützow* finally managed to make
contact with the convoy but could only
inflict splinter damage on one of its ships
before the destroyers forced her away.
With obvious relief her captain received
orders from Kummetz to rejoin the
flagship, and although there was one
more brief exchange of fire with the
British cruisers the German force

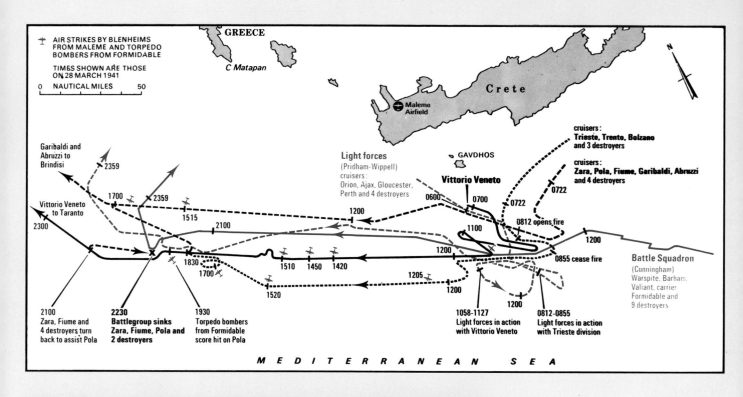

AIR STRIKES BY BLENHEIMS FROM MALEME AND TORPEDO BOMBERS FROM FORMIDABLE

TIMES SHOWN ARE THOSE ON 28 MARCH 1941

0   NAUTICAL MILES   50

GREECE

C Matapan

Crete

Maleme Airfield

Garibaldi and Abruzzi to Brindisi — 2359

1700   2359

1515

Vittorio Veneto to Taranto 2300

2100   1830   1700

Light forces (Pridham-Wippell) cruisers: Orion, Ajax, Gloucester, Perth and 4 destroyers

GAVDHOS

Vittorio Veneto

0600   0700   0722

0812 opens fire

1100

1200

0855 cease fire

cruisers: **Trieste, Trento, Bolzano** and 3 destroyers

cruisers: **Zara, Pola, Fiume, Garibaldi, Abruzzi** and 4 destroyers

0722

1200

Battle Squadron (Cunningham) Warspite, Barham, Valiant, carrier Formidable and 9 destroyers

1510   1450   1420

1205   1200

1520   1200

1200

2100 Zara, Fiume and 4 destroyers turn back to assist Pola

2230 Battlegroup sinks Zara, Fiume, Pola and 2 destroyers

1930 Torpedo bombers from Formidable score hit on Pola

1058-1127 Light forces in action with Vittorio Veneto

0812-0855 Light forces in action with Trieste division

MEDITERRANEAN SEA

Above: *The Battle of Cape Matapan.*

Left: *Quarterdeck of the* Penelope, *having her battle damage repaired in New York Navy Yard in August 1942.*

escaped to the west. Admiral Burnett had no intention of being lured away from the convoy, being content to have his two light cruisers put to flight a pair of ships armed with 8-inch and 11-inch guns.

To the British the Barents Sea action was a welcome antidote to the record of losses incurred by previous Russian convoys but to the Germans it was nothing less than a disgrace. When Hitler heard the news he gave way to paroxysms of rage punctuated by denunciations of the Navy. An order to lay up the big ships, strip their guns for coastal defence and use their armour plate for tanks provoked the resignation of the Commander-in-Chief, Admiral Raeder. Although this order was subsequently modified to allow the bulk of the ships to serve in the Baltic training squadron and the rest to remain in Norway to tie down British ships, this marked the beginning of the end for the German surface fleet.

The *Tirpitz* was never brought to action in the open sea but the battle-cruiser *Scharnhorst* made one final attempt to destroy a Murmansk convoy. It was almost exactly a year after the

Barents Sea *débâcle* but the results were even more disastrous, despite the fact that the new Commander-in-Chief, Admiral Dönitz, had demanded full freedom of action from Hitler. Once again the convoy's cruiser escort saved the day, with the *Belfast*, *Sheffield* and *Norfolk* engaging the *Scharnhorst* without regard for the risk. An 8-inch shell from the *Norfolk* destroyed the battle-cruiser's forward radar gunnery set, and all the time she was trying to work her way around the cruisers the Home Fleet was coming up in support. This time the covering force included the battleship *Duke of York*, whose 14-inch salvoes blasted the *Scharnhorst* and inflicted serious damage. Although destroyers then slowed her down with torpedoes it was left to the cruisers *Belfast* and *Jamaica* to finish her off. Two torpedoes from the *Jamaica* vanished into the pall of smoke that marked the position of the last ocean raider.

The Mediterranean

Much was hoped for from the fast Italian cruisers but they got off to an inauspicious start. On 19 July 1940 the *Bartolomeo Colleoni* and *Giovanni delle Bande Nere* were attacked by the Australian cruiser *Sydney* and her five escorting destroyers. Although the Italians had been credited with 37 knots their sea speed was only 30 knots, and so it came as something of a surprise to the *Sydney*'s captain to find that he was overhauling the enemy. During the long-range gunnery duel which followed, the *Sydney*'s 6-inch salvoes hit and disabled the *Bartolomeo Colleoni* but her consort escaped.

The theory that armoured 8-inch gun cruisers were a substitute for battleships was shown to be woefully wrong at the Battle of Cape Matapan on the night of 28 March 1941. The *Pola* was hit by aircraft torpedo while screening the damaged battleship *Vittorio Veneto*. In the hope of towing the *Pola* back to port, Admiral Iachino sent her two sisters back to look for her after dark. By a series of coincidences the three ships were caught together by the British Commander-in-Chief, Admiral Andrew Browne Cunningham, leading his force of three battleships. In the merciless glare of searchlights the *Fiume* and *Zara* were destroyed by 15-inch salvoes at less than 4000 yards. Then his destroyers finished off the crippled *Pola* and two destroyers. It was a victory which curbed any initiative the Italian

Above: *The luckless heavy cruiser* Pola, *whose torpedo damage led to the destruction of her sisters* Zara *and* Fiume *as well.*

Below: *The forward 6-inch guns of HMS* Penelope *showing new 20mm guns, radar and mast fittings.*

135

Navy had had, so that only two months later the British were left to complete the evacuation of Greece and Crete under only fierce air attack rather than a combined air-and-sea assault.

In fact the air assault was deadly by itself. The evacuation of Crete cost the Royal Navy dear, particularly in cruisers. At first things seemed to go well, despite the crippling of the *York* by Italian explosive motor boats in Suda Bay. On the night of 21 May 1941 the *Dido, Ajax* and *Orion* and four destroyers wiped out an invasion convoy bound for Crete in commandeered fishing craft. However the next day Stuka dive bombers sank the *Gloucester* and the *Fiji* after they had fired away all their 4-inch AA ammunition. Thereafter cruisers were warned not to allow their reserves of AA shells to fall below 40 per cent.

The anti-aircraft cruisers came into their own in the Mediterranean, where their lower endurance did not matter. Losses were particularly heavy, *Calypso, Cairo, Naiad, Bonaventure* and *Hermione* were torpedoed and *Coventry, Calcutta* and *Spartan* were sunk by air attack. In addition the *Carlisle* was so badly damaged by Italian bombers in Scarpanto Strait that she was laid up at Alexandria and never repaired. Many cruisers were damaged by air and submarine attack, and in all 17 were lost (see table opposite).

Below: *HMS* Sheffield *at Gibraltar on her way out to the Mediterranean in August 1940.*

Calypso	Torpedoed by Italian submarine 12 June 1940
Southampton	Bombed 10 January 1941 and then scuttled
Bonaventure	Torpedoed by Italian submarine 31 March 1941
York	Damaged by motor boats, beached and bombed 22 April – 22 May 1941, then abandoned
Gloucester	Bombed off Crete 22 May 1941
Fiji	Bombed off Crete 22 May 1941
Calcutta	Bombed north-west of Alexandria 1 June 1941
Galatea	Torpedoed by U-Boat off Alexandria 15 December 1941
Neptune	Mined off Tripoli 19 December 1941
Naiad	Torpedoed by U-Boat off Crete 11 March 1942
Hermione	Torpedoed by U-Boat north of Sollum 16 June 1942
Cairo	Torpedoed by Italian submarine 12 August 1942
Manchester	Torpedoed by Italian Motor Torpedo Boats 13 August 1942
Coventry	Bombed off Tobruk 14 September 1942
Carlisle	Bombed 9 October 1943 and written-off
Spartan	Bombed off Anzio 29 January 1944
Penelope	Torpedoed by U-Boat off Anzio 18 February 1944

Perhaps the most famous of these was HMS *Penelope*. While she was based on Malta as part of a striking force (Force 'K') she was subjected to heavy air attack. While in dock to repair damage, her hull was pitted with so many splinter holes that she was nicknamed HMS 'Pepperpot'. With her sister *Aurora* and the destroyers *Lance* and *Lively* she struck at the Italian convoys carrying fuel to the Axis forces in North Africa. Although Malta was badly exposed to air attack from bases in Sicily the cruisers and destroyers took a steady toll of shipping and contributed to the final collapse of the Afrika Korps in 1942.

The Italians were also suffering steady attrition from British aircraft and submarines. The old armoured cruiser *San Giorgio* was sunk by bombing at Tobruk and the *Trieste* and *Muzio Attendolo* were sunk at their moorings by bombing. The *Trento*, *Giovanni delle Bande Nere* and *Armando Diaz* were torpedoed by submarines and the *Gorizia*, *Bolzano*, *Taranto* (formerly the German *Strassburg*) and *Bari* (formerly the German *Pillau*) fell into German hands at the time of the Italian Armistice in September 1943. In addition the *Alberto de Giussano* and *Alberico da Barbiano* were sunk in a night action by British and Dutch destroyers off Cape Bon. The disaster was compounded because the two cruisers were carrying an inflammable cargo of petrol on deck, intended for the Army in North Africa; both ships burst into flame immediately and sank with heavy loss of life. It transpired that the Italian Naval HQ had told Admiral Toscano of the presence of four Allied destroyers, but it was considered that they would never dare attack two fast cruisers with their own destroyer escort.

Cruisers played their final part in the Mediterranean Campaign in 1944 when they supported the Allied landings at Anzio. As they had shown in the 'Torch' landings in North Africa and were to show in Normandy later that year, cruisers were ideal for providing fire support. Although lacking the range of battleships they drew less water and could be risked in places where a prestigious capital ship could not. Also their high speed gave them a measure of immunity against counter-attacks from enemy shore batteries. It was a pattern which was to be repeated 30 years later.

Above right: The heavy cruiser Trieste *at sea in 1940–41. She originally had level tops to her funnels.*

Below: The heavy cruiser HMS York *dips to a heavy swell off Gibraltar in August 1940. Eight months later she was a beached wreck at Suda Bay, Crete.*

Above: *The old armoured cruiser San Giorgio, a twisted and burning wreck in Tobruk, 22 January 1941. She had been converted into a coast defence ship in 1937–38.*

The Pacific and Far East

If the struggle between Fascism and Democracy began long before the outbreak of the World War II the struggle between the United States and the Japanese Empire cast its shadow equally far ahead. Yet, although the invasion of China strained relations between the two countries, and in spite of attacks on British and American gunboats on the Yangtze and other incidents, the peace held until 7 December 1941.

Although the first cruisers in action were the USS *Honolulu* and *Raleigh*, attacked at Pearl Harbor, and the old Japanese armoured cruiser *Idzumo* which sank the British gunboat *Peterel* at Shanghai, the first proper cruiser actions took place in the East Indies. A hurriedly organised American—British—Dutch—Australian (ABDA) joint command was set up to defend the East Indies against the Japanese invasion but it was at best a belated ramshackle arrangement, with too few ships, planes and men. When the Dutch naval commander, Admiral Karel Doorman tried to stop the Japanese in the Makassar Strait on 4 February 1942 his three cruisers came under heavy air attack. The flagship *de*

Ruyter escaped with only minor damage but the USS *Houston* had her after 8-inch turret destroyed and the *Marblehead* was hit in her steering gear. The ABDA force withdrew to Tjilatjap having achieved nothing.

Admiral Doorman did his best to fight back, and on 19 February his forces engaged the Japanese off Bali in the Battle of Badoeng Strait. He had the *de Ruyter* and *Java* with three destroyers in one group and the *Tromp* and four destroyers in another, facing Admiral Kubo in the light cruiser *Nagara* and three destroyers escorting a force of transports carrying troops to Bali. The *Nagara* took no part in the action as she was escorting a damaged transport, and so when the two forces made contact at

1100 there were only three Japanese destroyers facing the *de Ruyter* and *Java* and their three destroyers. In the confused action which followed the Dutch *Piet Hein* was torpedoed without any loss to the Japanese. Then the second ABDA group arrived, the *Tromp* and her four American destroyers. Without even a common codebook the newcomers could not identify the recognition signals being flashed at them, and so they could make very little contribution to the battle. The light cruiser *Tromp* was badly knocked about, with 11 hits in her superstructure from the destroyer *Asashio*, while the *Michishio* was hit repeatedly by the USS *John D Edwards* and the other two destroyers were lightly damaged.

Below: *The light cruiser* Raleigh *listing badly, after the Pearl Harbor attack, kept afloat by two salvage pontoons lashed alongside. She had been hit by an aircraft torpedo.*

Above: *The* Tama *in 1942, wearing a camouflage scheme. She was torpedoed by a US submarine off Cape Engaño during the Battle of Leyte Gulf, a fate which overtook her sisters* Kuma *and* Oi.

Above: *The* Ashigara *in 1929. In 1934–35 she was modernised with twin 5-inch AA guns.*

Doorman was deprived of the *Tromp*, which returned to Australia for repairs, but by mid-February he had been reinforced by the British *Exeter*, repaired and modernised after the Battle of the River Plate, the *Dragon* and *Danae*, the Australian *Hobart* and *Perth* and the USS *Houston*, *Marblehead* and *Boise*. Against him were ranged a force of carriers, seaplane tenders and destroyers, as well as the heavy cruisers *Nachi*, *Haguro*, *Myoko*, *Maya*, *Atago*, *Takao*, *Chokai*, *Mikuma*, *Mogami*, *Suzuya* and *Kumano* and the light cruisers *Jintsu*, *Nagara*, *Naka* and *Yura*. Not all these ships were concentrated for the Battle of the Java Sea on 27 February which spelled the end of the ABDA force.

The Allied ships were completely out-fought and the result was never in doubt. The ships were outclassed and their crews were exhausted. The destruction began at 1638 when the *Exeter* was set on fire by an 8-inch shell from the *Nachi* and minutes later the destroyer *Kortenaer* blew up from a torpedo hit. Doorman broke away, having failed to get at the invasion transports which had been his main target, but his force was in a sorry state. The *Exeter* was still blazing but managed to hold a straight course parallel to the southeast in company with four destroyers, the other cruisers formed themselves into a second column about 10,000 yards away. But the Japanese were not going to let them go and by 1715 they were in range again, firing 8-inch salvoes and torpedoes. The *Exeter* was now making only five knots and she was the target chosen by the *Jintsu* and *Naka* and their destroyers. Only the bravery of her escorting destroyers *Electra* and *Encounter* saved her from the first attack by two destroyers, and although the *Electra* was

sunk the cruiser managed to limp back to Surabaya.

The rest of the force were not so fortunate. Later that night the *de Ruyter* was torpedoed by the *Nachi* and *Haguro*, sinking with Admiral Doorman and 344 officers and men on board. Four minutes later the *Java* also burst into flames after a torpedo hit, leaving only the *Houston* and *Perth* to make their way back to Batavia as best they could. Now it was *sauve qui peut* as all units tried to escape to Australia or Ceylon. The *Exeter* and *Encounter* were hunted down by the *Ashigara* and *Myoko* on 1 March, while the same day saw the end of the *Houston* and *Perth*. However they wrote a magnificent ending to the story of ABDA by charging the Japanese invasion transports lying in Bantam Bay. For a while confusion reigned and the Japanese destroyers fired at one another in their haste to fend off the two Allied cruisers. Although both ships paid the inevitable price, the transports had been damaged, although mainly by Japanese shells and torpedoes.

The same Japanese carriers under Admiral Nagumo which had devastated Pearl Harbor now turned their attention to the British in the Indian Ocean. In a devastating strike on Colombo his carrier planes bombed the harbour and hit several ships. A chance sighting by a floatplane from the heavy cruiser *Tone* called down another strike on the heavy cruisers *Dorsetshire* and *Cornwall* hurrying south to join the main fleet at Addu Attoll. The two ships were overwhelmed by the 88 planes and sank within 20 minutes.

Above: *The* Nachi *in 1933–34, shortly before she started her modernisation in February 1935. She was sunk by planes off Corregidor in November 1944.*

So far all had gone in favour of the Japanese but the Battles of the Coral Sea and Midway brought their headlong advance under control. Cruisers played no special role in these two carrier battles but they demonstrated their efficiency as screening ships for the carriers, with ample speed to keep up with them and providing a heavy AA battery. At Midway the Japanese deployed seven cruisers while the Americans had eight (including two Australian ships). Only when the fight-

Above: *The new American AA cruiser* Atlanta *on trials in 1942. She was crippled by gunfire during the Battle of Guadalcanal on 13 November 1942.*

ing shifted to the Solomons in August 1942 did cruisers come into their own.

Guadalcanal is no more than a mountainous, malarial island at the bottom end of the Solomons but it lay astride the route of the Japanese thrust towards New Guinea and Australia. The Americans were alarmed by a report at the beginning of May 1942 that a seaplane base was being built at Tulagi, north of Guadalcanal, but news two months later that Japanese engineers were building an airfield at Lunga Point on Guadalcanal brought an immediate response. On 7 August the US Marines stormed ashore to seize the new airfield; whoever held it had the key to the Solomons, and for the next six months

it was the scene of some of the bloodiest fighting of World War II. As long as the airstrip – now christened Henderson Field – was in US hands all Japanese forces could be attacked within a 250-mile radius. Equally, in Japanese hands it would make naval operations in support of the Marines all but impossible.

It was made quite clear that the Japanese would spare no effort to dislodge the Americans. The day after the landings a force of five heavy and two light cruisers under Admiral Mikawa left Rabaul for Guadalcanal, intent on smashing their way through the Allied warships in Savo Sound to allow six fast transports to land re-inforcements on

Guadalcanal. By a series of mischances, sightings of Mikawa's force by bombers and submarines were not relayed to the commander of the force of Allied cruisers lying off Savo Island, Vice-Admiral Victor Crutchley RN. On the morning of 9 August Australian planes spotted Mikawa twice off Bougainville; the message was not transmitted until the afternoon, and then took eight hours to reach the British and American commanders. Nor did the two patrolling destroyers spot the Japanese cruisers gliding past in the dark.

When Mikawa's cruisers attacked at 0143 they had the Allied cruisers at their mercy. In the light of flares dropped by floatplanes they riddled the Australian *Canberra* with 8-inch shellfire and then torpedoed her. Four minutes after that the *Chicago* had her bow blown off by a torpedo. Moving north the Japanese now dealt with the USS *Quincy*, *Astoria* and *Vincennes* in turn. Surprise was complete and only the *Quincy* managed to retaliate; she hit the *Chokai* three times before sinking. The Japanese ships vanished as silently as they had arrived, leaving carnage behind them. Two thousand men were dead or injured, four heavy cruisers were sunk and one badly damaged in return for only slight damage to the flagship *Chokai*. The only comfort that the Allies could draw from the Battle of Savo Island was Mikawa's failure to sink any of the troop transports lying off Lunga Point and the sinking of the heavy cruiser *Kako* by an American submarine 70 miles off Kavieng during the run back to Rabaul.

The Japanese Navy continued to do its utmost to help the Army, running troops in under cover of darkness and bombarding Henderson Field at night. These fast runs down the island chain from Rabaul soon became known as the 'Tokyo Express' and under Rear-Admiral Raizo Tanaka they were conducted with audacity and skill. Without the benefit of radar the Japanese lookouts could still be relied on to make the first sighting, and their designers' wisdom in providing the cruisers with torpedoes gave them a great advantage in close-range action. Above all it was the attention paid to night-fighting tactics that gave the Japanese the edge in so many of these actions.

In October 1942 the Americans decided to run a convoy of their own reinforcements into Guadalcanal, and this brought on a near disaster off Cape Esperance on the night of 11–12 October. To protect the convoy the US Navy mustered a distant covering force of a battleship and a carrier but close escort was entrusted to Task Force 64 under Rear-Admiral Norman Scott, with the heavy cruisers *San Francisco* and *Salt Lake City* and the light cruisers *Boise* and *Helena*, with five destroyers. The Americans fully expected the Japanese to try to stop the convoy but in fact its arrival had gone undetected. What the Japanese were intending, however, was a night bombardment of Henderson Field by three heavy cruisers and two destroyers. As the Americans had foreknowledge of their time of arrival they were confident that they could get their revenge for Savo Island.

At 2235 Admiral Scott formed his force into line ahead, three destroyers leading the four cruisers and two more bringing up the rear. The Japanese Admiral Goto's force was also in line ahead formation but with a destroyer on either beam of the leading cruiser. Both sides made mistakes; Goto's lookouts sighted a burning floatplane but the Japanese commander did not interpret the information correctly, while the *Helena* picked up the Japanese force on her SG radar but failed to report the sighting for another 15 minutes. The Americans had hoped to use their cruisers' floatplanes to drop illuminating flares as the Japanese had at Savo Island but the performance was disappointing and they provided little useful information. What information did reach the flagship was garbled, so the tactical advantage was largely thrown away.

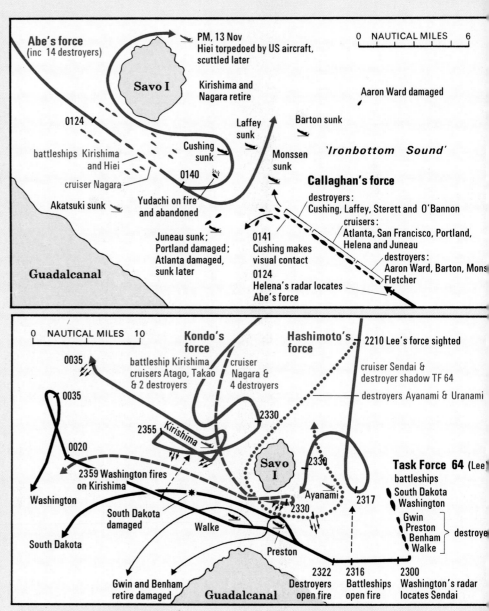

Above: *Two stages of the Battle of Guadalcanal.*

Below: *The heavy cruiser USS Pensacola in September 1942, showing her radar antennae. Although outclassed by the Japanese night-fighting techniques the Americans were ultimately able to turn the tables with radar-controlled gunfire.*

Below: *The anti-aircraft cruiser San Juan had the massive armament of eight twin 5-inch gun mountings and eight torpedo tubes, but the displacement proved too small. Later ships of this class sacrificed the torpedoes and two gun mountings.*

Below: *The USS Portland in dry dock at Cockatoo Island Dockyard, Sydney in 1942. The great distances steamed in the Pacific imposed great strain on ships, and as the war went on forward bases had to be extemporised in remote anchorages.*

At 2346 the *Helena* opened fire with her 6-inch and 5-inch guns on the flagship *Aoba* and the destroyer *Duncan* started to fire her 5-inch at the *Furutaka*. Admiral Goto was mortally wounded and the *Furutaka* was set on fire but the other cruiser, the *Kinugasa*, and the destroyer *Hatsuyuki* managed to obey Goto's last order to reverse course, and escaped serious damage. The Japanese were still very dangerous, and at midnight the *Kinugasa* surprised the *Salt Lake City* with uncomfortably accurate salvoes at 8000 yards. Then the *Boise* was hit four times and was only saved when the *Salt Lake City* steamed between her and the Japanese ships. The *Boise* was lucky to escape, for an 8-inch shell penetrated No 1 triple 6-inch turret and a 6-inch shell (from another US ship) caused a bad explosion in her forward magazines.

The *Furutaka* finally sank after many hits, 'Abandon ship' was piped at 0220 hours. The *Aoba*, however, survived an estimated 40 hits from 6-inch and 8-inch shells and was still making 30 knots at the end of the action, and the *Kinugasa* had only trifling damage. It had been a scrappy, inconclusive battle but both sides had achieved their main objective of getting their troops safely ashore.

The next major action, the Battle of Guadalcanal on 13–14 November, did not go well for the Americans. On the first night the heavy cruisers *San Francisco* and *Portland*, the light cruiser *Helena* and the anti-aircraft cruisers *Atlanta* and *Juneau* ran into a force which included the fast battleships *Hiei* and *Kirishima* and the light cruiser *Nagara*.

Above: *The light cruiser* Nashville *bombarding Kiska in the Aleutians in August 1942.*

Once again it was the *Helena*'s efficient SG radar set which detected the enemy but she was positioned towards the rear of the column, a difficult position for it to function effectively. Once again poor radio discipline overloaded the voice net with messages, with the result that Rear-Admiral Callaghan could make little sense out of the reports.

The *mêlée* which ensued has been described as the most confused and horrifying naval action of the entire war. Admiral Callaghan's force did not know that it had charged right into the middle of the Japanese force until the *Atlanta* was illuminated by the searchlights of the *Hiei* and the destroyer *Akatsuki*. The battleship's 14-inch shells ripped into the flimsy superstructure of the *Atlanta*, killing Admiral Scott. She was then torpedoed, having managed to fire only one salvo of 5-inch shells. However the two Japanese ships immediately drew a hail of fire from the American destroyers and drew away; the *Akatsuki* was sunk shortly afterwards and the *Hiei*'s upperworks were set on fire. In the confusion the *San Francisco* started to fire on the *Atlanta* but soon realised her mistake, but only seconds later she herself was hit by 14-inch salvoes from the *Kirishima* and 5-inch fire from two destroyers. The *San Francisco*'s bridge was destroyed and Admiral Callaghan and his staff were killed.

The battle now degenerated into a sort of dogfight. Admiral Abe in the burning *Hiei* had lost control of his ships and the two American admirals were dead. Individual ships fired at whatever targets they could see. In these conditions the Japanese were more likely to win, thanks to their superior training. The *Nagara* and the destroyers sank the destroyer *Barton*, crippled the *Portland*

Below: *A stern view of the* Nashville *firing her 6-inch guns against Kiska.*

with a torpedo and set the AA cruiser *Juneau* on fire, before raking the *San Francisco* with gunfire. The *Helena* gave a good account of herself at first, using radar-controlled gunfire to drive off the *Amatsukaze* but she was then badly mauled by three more Japanese destroyers. When the firing died away at 0200 two Japanese destroyers and the *Hiei* were doomed (she would be sunk the next day by land-based and carrier aircraft) but the Americans had lost two destroyers and an AA cruiser and had several badly damaged. The *San Francisco* and *Helena* lived to fight another day but next day the battered *Juneau* was torpedoed by a Japanese submarine and two more destroyers had to be abandoned.

It had been a desperate affair and the US Navy held a long and searching post-mortem on its tactics and methods of command. Against the losses could be set the failure of the Japanese to effect their planned bombardment of Henderson Field. Another battle was fought the following night between two US battleships and a Japanese force comprising the *Kirishima* and the cruisers *Sendai*, *Nagara*, *Atago* and *Takao*. Once again there was confusion but the Americans got the better of the exchange, and the *Kirishima* was sunk by 16-inch shellfire from the *Washington*. Aircraft from Henderson Field had also caught Admiral Mikawa's bombardment force at daybreak the day before, sinking the *Kinugasa* and damaging the *Chokai*, *Maya* and *Isuzu*. Not even the Japanese could go on accepting losses on this scale and when an air strike devastated the reinforcement convoy brought in by 'Tenacious Tanaka' on 14 November it was the beginning of the end. Although the 'Tokyo Express' continued to run there was no longer any hope of supporting the Army by bringing on a full-scale naval battle. From now on the Japanese would be in retreat.

There were to be other battles in the Solomons but they were fought around the 'Tokyo Express', which began to reverse the process by steadily evacuating the garrison from Guadalcanal. The

Below: *The Chicago sinking off Rennell Island on 30 January 1943.*

Below: *The heavy cruiser* Salt Lake City *at Brisbane in 1942. She is wearing an unusual camouflage scheme with a false bow wave, but she has not yet received any radar.*

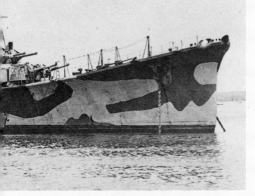

Below: *The* Myoko *lying at Singapore with two German U-Boats alongside.*

Battle of Tassafaronga on the night of 30 November to 1 December showed that even if the Americans ruled the sea by day the Japanese ruled at night. Four US cruisers, the *Minneapolis*, *New Orleans*, *Pensacola* and *Northampton* were torpedoed in quick succession by eight destroyers under Tanaka's command. Good damage control saved three of them but the *Northampton* caught fire and had to be abandoned.

Much of the Japanese success in these night actions depended on the long accurate running of the 24-inch 'Long Lance' torpedo, to which there was no effective answer at first. Eventually cruisers provided the solution, using their 6-inch and 8-inch guns with radar-control to lay down barrage fire at maximum range. This technique was used by Rear-Admiral Merrill in the Battle of Empress Augusta Bay on the night of 2 November 1943. The new light cruisers of the *Cleveland* Class were coming forward, armed with twelve 6-inch guns and equipped with the latest fire-control radar. The rapid fire of the

6-inch was better suited to this sort of action than the 8-inch, and so the new *Baltimore* Class were more usually allocated to the carrier task forces.

Once the United States and other Allied forces broke out of the Solomons and demolished the so-called 'Bismarck Barrier' the role of cruisers in supporting destroyer forces took second place to the less glamorous roles of carrier escort and shore bombardment. As ever the cruiser could make up in numbers for the small number of battleships and there was no diminution of their importance. The US Navy had started an enormous programme of cruiser construction early in 1942 to supplement the 1940 'Two-Ocean Navy' programme. Three basic types were in hand, the *Cleveland* Class light cruisers, the *Baltimore* Class heavy cruisers and also the *Atlanta* Class anti-aircraft cruisers.

The 10,000-ton *Clevelands* were a development of the pre-war *Brooklyns*, sacrificing the redundant fifth triple 6-inch turret for a heavier AA battery of six twin 5-inch guns. They set a new

Below: *The USS* Minneapolis *(CA-36) at Espiritu Santa in January 1943 being fitted with a temporary bow.*

record as the largest single class of cruisers ever ordered. Even allowing for nine converted on the slipways to light aircraft carriers (CVLs) 30 ships were completed between 1940 and the end of the war. The *Baltimore* Class resembled the *Clevelands* in being flush-decked with two slim capped funnels but their designers were now free of the 10,000 ton limit and so they rose to 13,600 tons – proof that the original limit had been too small for a balanced design.

These two classes were a logical progression from previous US cruisers but the third class marked a radical departure. The *Atlanta* Class resembled the British *Dido* Class AA cruisers in being much smaller (6000 tons) than the standard 'fleet' cruiser. Unlike the British ships they were originally intended to work with destroyers to neutralise the advantage of the big Special Type destroyers built by the Japanese. Although also intended to fulfil a fleet AA defence role with the massive armament of eight twin 5-inch dual-purpose gun mountings (three forward, two on the beam and three aft) their main role was to act as a type of destroyer-leader. In fact the provision of so many guns with only two high-angle directors was shown by war experience to be a mistake. They were originally intended to make 38 knots to allow them to catch Japanese destroyers but so much extra weight was incorporated that they were never good for more than 33 knots in service. They were heavily overloaded and when a repeat class was ordered in 1942, the *Oakland* Class, the beam 5-inch guns were suppressed. This was still not enough and in the second group the torpedo tubes were suppressed and the second and fifth 5-inch turrets were moved down one deck.

Providing more and more AA guns was a constant headache. In the pre-war heavy cruiser *Indianapolis* topweight was at such a premium that it was proposed to remove two quadruple 40-mm Bofors mountings to allow Admiral Nimitz and his staff to embark. The Commander-in-Chief expressed his amazement at the narrow margin of stability, but it must be remembered that the Washington Treaty cruisers had been built to very fine limits and wartime additions had not been made with caution. When faced with a massive

Right: *The USS* Portland *recovering her SOC Seagull floatplane in 1944. The Seagull is approaching the landing mat.*

Top: *The* Cleveland, *first of the new light cruisers, at sea in 1942.*

Above: *The light cruiser* Boise *shelling New Guinea in February 1943.*

that when the *Essex* Class 33 knot carriers were being planned in 1939 there were no capital ships capable of escorting them at top speed. There would be the 33-knot *Iowa* Class battleships from 1943-44 but it was envisaged that these would be fully occupied in the battle fleet, fighting against their Japanese opposite numbers. So a very fast long-range cruiser with guns ranging out to 11,000 yards made some sense, but what resulted was a very expensive ship of limited utility. Only two were completed, the *Alaska* and *Guam* in 1944, and although they proved magnificent steamers they never justified the colossal effort which went into building them. A third ship was never completed and three more were cancelled in 1943 to conserve steel.

Two more designs were prepared during the war, and although they were not completed until much later they show how far the cruiser could be taken. The first was an expansion of the single-funnelled *Oregon City*, the improved *Baltimore* Class. On a displacement of 17,000 tons the armament of the *Des Moines* Class remained as nine 8-inch guns but the extra weight was used to provide fully automatic loading for the guns. The Mark XVI 8-inch 55-calibre gun fired shells with wrapped charges at a range of 10 per minute, about four times as fast as earlier marks of 8-inch, and the mounting allowed elevation of up to 41 degrees. Without doubt these ships were the most powerful cruisers ever designed (excepting such freaks as the *Alaska* Class) capable of delivering a heavy volume of fire up to 14 miles away. With new automatic twin 3-inch close-range AA mountings, each with its own radar control, and four more directors for the 5-inch guns the weight of AA fire exceeded that of battleships. The only drawback to such a ship was her size, which took her almost into the category of a capital ship and thus limited her usefulness.

The *Worcester* Class, at 14,700 tons, ran the *Des Moines* Class a close second but it was intended to be an expansion of the *Oakland* Class AA cruisers, using a new dual-purpose automatic 6-inch 47-calibre twin mounting in place of the 5-inch 38-calibre. These mountings could fire a 130lb projectile to a height of 48,000 feet at 78 degrees elevation or out to a range of just over 26,000 yards. In layout this class was almost identical to the original *Oakland*, with three turrets forward and three aft, the fore-

weight of air attack any sailor will trade seaworthiness for firepower.

The requirements of AA firepower were paramount in the Pacific and the US Navy was fortunate to have a reliable 40mm mounting with its own gyro sight, backed up by single (and later twin) hand-operated 20mm Oerlikons. Both the *Baltimore* and *Cleveland* Classes were revised to combine the uptakes into one funnel, purely to allow a more rational layout of the close-range AA armament, and by the end of the war catapults and floatplanes were being discarded. In the early days they had provided useful reconnaissance for long-range gunfire but these functions had been largely taken over by radar.

There is one more class of American cruisers to be mentioned. This is the somewhat freakish *Alaska* Class, displacing 29,000 tons and armed with nine 12-inch guns. Although loosely referred to as battlecruisers they bore no resemblance to the original type and were always rated by the US Navy as large cruisers (CB). For many years it was believed that the class had been designed to match a class of Japanese ships rumoured to be building – the *Chichibu* Class. This did not exist but the *Alaska* Class was not built purely as a result of an erroneous intelligence assessment. It came about as a result of somewhat morbid fears that the 8-inch gun would not be adequate to secure protection for fast carriers from attack by enemy cruisers. It must be remembered

Below: *The new heavy cruiser Baltimore in 1944 was armed with nine 8-inch guns and a dozen 5-inch AA guns.*

Right: *The heavy cruiser USS Northampton in action against Wotje Atoll in February 1942.*

Below: *Crewmen clean salt and ice from a quadruple Bofors AA mounting on board the Salt Lake City in March 1943.*

Right: *The badly blistered 8-inch guns of the Salt Lake City after the Battle of the Komandorski Islands in March 1943.*

most and aftermost at the same level to keep down topweight. The biggest headache with this class of ships was manpower as they had so many mountings. They were planned to have 11 twin and two single 3-inch guns, in addition to their seven 6-inch turrets, and the wartime complement would have been 1700 officers and men. They would have been formidable opponents but would have lacked that essential feature of cruisers – expendability.

The exertions of the United States' shipbuilding industry in World War II now seems almost unbelievable. The following tables give some idea of the vast cruiser programme (see table).

As the end of the war approached the cruiser programme began to slow down to release shipyard resources for landing craft. In 1944-45 35 cruisers of all types were cancelled for the US Navy now had as many as it could man. Even so several were not completed until some time after the war was over.

The US Navy took the cruiser to its ultimate in 1941-45, producing ships of unparalleled fighting power. What characterised American cruisers was their uniformity of equipment and massive anti-aircraft armaments. Although other classes of warships had their virtues it could be argued that the US Navy had more conspicuous success with its bigger cruiser designs than anyone else. Their Washington Treaty designs set them on the right road, and right through to 1945 there was little need to make more than minor improvements. The Japanese cruisers, by comparison, showed more ingenuity but caused their designers many headaches. Nothing like the disastrous story of the *Mogami* Class happened in the US Navy and apart from a premature abandonment of torpedo tubes the designs met wartime requirements.

Although the arguments against 8-inch guns had some validity, the arrival of radar on the scene finally justified the choice. With radar-controlled gunnery hits could be obtained at maximum range and therefore the extra range of the 8-inch gun was more likely to be decisive. However it was in their high endurance and mechanical reliability that American cruisers showed real superiority over all others. As had been foreseen way back in 1919 the battleground was to be the Pacific and ships would have to steam immense distances. The dollars invested in machinery and boiler improvements were well spent.

Name	No	Built
14 Baltimore Class		
Baltimore	(CA.68)	1941–43
Boston	(CA.69)	1941–43
Canberra[1]	(CA.70)	1941–43
Quincy	(CA.71)	1941–43
Pittsburgh	(CA.72)	1943–44
St Paul	(CA.73)	1943–45
Columbus	(CA.74)	1943–45
Helena	(CA.75)	1943–45
Bremerton	(CA.130)	1943–45
Fall River	(CA.131)	1943–45
Macon	(CA.132)	1943–45
Toledo	(CA.133)	1943–45
Los Angeles	(CA.135)	1943–45
Chicago	(CA.136)	1943–45

[1]renamed in honour of HMAS *Canberra* after Savo Island

Name	No	Built
3 Oregon City Class[2]		
Oregon City	(CA.122)	1944–46
Albany	(CA.123)	1944–46
Rochester	(CA.124)	1944–46

[2]single funnelled version of *Baltimore* Class

Name	No	Built
3 Des Moines Class[3]		
Des Moines	(CA.134)	1945–48
Salem	(CA.139)	1945–49
Newport News	(CA.148)	1945–49

[3]expanded version of *Oregon City* with automatic 8-inch guns

Name	No	Built
36 Cleveland Class		
Cleveland	(CL.55)	1940–42
Columbia	(CL.56)	1940–42
Montpelier	(CL.57)	1940–42
Denver	(CL.58)	1940–42
Amsterdam (i)	(CL.59)	converted to carrier
Santa Fé	(CL.60)	1941–42
Tallahassee	(CL.61)	converted to carrier
Birmingham	(CL.62)	1941–43
Mobile	(CL.63)	1941–43
Vincennes	(CL.64)	1942–44
Pasadena	(CL.65)	1943–44
Springfield	(CL.66)	1943–44
Topeka	(CL.67)	1943–44

Name	No	Built
New Haven	(CL.76)	converted to carrier
Huntingdon (i)	(CL.77)	converted to carrier
Dayton	(CL.78)	converted to carrier
Wilmington	(CL.79)	converted to carrier
Biloxi	(CL.79)	1941-43
Houston	(CL.80)	1941-43
Providence	(CL.81)	1943-45
Manchester	(CL.82)	1944-46
Fargo (i)	(CL.84)	converted to carrier
Vicksburg	(CL.85)	1942-44
Duluth	(CL.87)	1942-44
Miami	(CL.89)	1941-43
Astoria	(CL.90)	1941-44
Oklahoma City	(CL.91)	1942-44
Little Rock	(CL.92)	1943-45
Galveston	(CL.93)	1944-46

Name	No	Built
Buffalo (ii)	(CL.99)	converted to carrier
Newark	(CL.100)	converted to carrier
Amsterdam (ii)	(CL.101)	1943-45
Portsmouth	(CL.102)	1943-45
Wilkes-Barre	(CL.103)	1942-44
Atlanta	(CL.104)	1943-44
Dayton	(CL.105)	1943-45

2 Fargo Class[4]

Name	No	Built
Fargo	(CL.106)	1943-45
Huntington (ii)	(CL.107)	1943-46

[4]single-funnelled version of *Cleveland* Class

4 Atlanta Class

Name	No	Built
Atlanta	(CL.51)	1940-41
Juneau (i)	(CL.52)	1940-42
San Diego	(CL.53)	1940-42
San Juan	(CL.54)	1940-42

7 Oakland Class

Name	No	Built
Oakland	(CL.95)	1941-43
Reno	(CL.96)	1941-43
Flint	(CL.97)	1942-44
Tucson	(CL.98)	1942-45
Juneau (ii)	(CL.119)	1944-46
Spokane	(CL.120)	1944-46
Fresno	(CL.121)	1945-46

2 Worcester Class

Name	No	Built
Worcester	(CL.144)	1945-48
Roanoke	(CL.145)	1945-48

2 Alaska Class

Name	No	Built
Alaska	(CB.1)	1941-44
Guam	(CB.2)	1942-44

Below: *The new Japanese light cruiser Noshiro running trials in June 1943. She and her sisters of the Agano Class were armed with three twin 5.9-inch gun turrets, four 3-inch AA guns and 32 25mm AA. They were built in 1940-44.*

The Decline of the gun

Night action is always spectacular. 'X' triple 6-inch turret in HMS Mauritius fires in support of the Fifth Army in Italy in 1943.

Even if the battleship had not been ousted from her position as the premier type of warship by the aircraft carrier, her running and manpower costs made her an anachronism. In the years after 1945 there was still a need for heavy gunpower, and this combined with her lower running costs kept the cruiser in favour for many years more.

The lessons of World War II, particularly in the Mediterranean and the Pacific, were that cruisers must have a much more powerful anti-aircraft armament than had ever been planned. The need was not so much for quantity as quality, many pre-war cruisers had an impressive number of barrels but had not been able to use all of them with equal effect. A prime example was the original *Atlanta* design, which theoretically had a powerful battery of fourteen 5-inch guns available on each broadside. However with only two Mark 37 fire control systems the ship could only engage two groups of aircraft with controlled fire, and experience showed that controlled fire was always more effective than a noisy barrage based on eye-shooting. Another example was the British *Edinburgh* Class, which had two more twin 4-inch AA mountings than the previous *Southampton* Class. Not only did the extra guns not have the

benefit of an extra fire-control system but they also received their ammunition from a common hoist 110 feet away. The German heavy cruisers, whatever other drawbacks they suffered from, set a good precedent in having a heavy secondary battery of six twin 10.5cm (4.1-inch) AA guns, served by four separate fire-control directors at the corners of the superstructure.

Positioning of guns was important. The most convenient position was in the waist, where it was not too difficult to find deck space. In the original *Brooklyn* Class, for example, the four unshielded 5-inch guns on each side were out in the open, with limited ammunition supplies by each gun. This was far from ideal, for a blast could knock out the entire battery and a series of attacks close together would use up ammunition before reserve supplies could be brought up from the magazines. In British cruisers from the *Leander* Class onwards the problem was met by grouping the guns in four positions around the funnel, where they were assured of a direct supply of ammunition. From the *Southampton* Class the twin 4-inch was made standard, with four mountings grouped around the second funnel and with a further refinement in the form of weatherproof shelters for the gun crews

between the mountings on either side. The value of this became obvious in wartime, when AA guns' crews could be kept 'closed up' for much longer periods than the men manning the main armament; even a place to sit and drink a mug of hot cocoa was better than standing next to a gun mounting exposed to the elements.

US cruisers adopted a different system. In two of the later *Brooklyn* Class, the *Helena* and *St Louis*, the eight guns were put into four twin enclosed mountings at the corners of the superstructure. Their contemporary, the heavy cruiser *Wichita*, had single 5-inch guns in enclosed mountings forward and aft of the superstructure firing over the 8-inch turrets, two more winged out on either side of the bridgework and four more unshielded guns in the waist. The final disposition adopted was a 'lozenge' formation, with a twin 5-inch mounting forward and aft on the centre-line and four at the corners of the superstructure. The twin 5-inch 38-calibre dual-purpose mounting, like the single, had its own ammunition supply and was fully enclosed to make it blast- and weatherproof.

War experience soon showed that aircraft preferred to attack ships from astern. Not only did this avoid the heavy

Left: *The* Wichita *looked like a* Brooklyn *Class light cruiser but was in fact the 18th heavy cruiser built under the Washington Treaty.*

Below: *The USS* Chester *off Mare Island Navy Yard in September 1943. She and her sisters were considerably modified, with funnel caps, radar and 40mm Bofors and 20mm Oerlikon light AA guns added in 1942–43.*

fire from the ship's guns mounted on the broadside but the wake provided a good mark to align the aircraft with on its run in. Attack from dead ahead was also dangerous for it usually preceded an attempt to machine-gun the bridge and knock out the nerve-centre of the ship. In British cruisers this was first countered by siting rocket-projectors, known as UP (Unrotating Projectile) mountings, on 'B' turret but these were soon replaced by single 20mm. Later, when they became available, 40mm Bofors guns were used. In most designs there was no room to do more, but the second group of the *Dido* Class were altered during construction to mount a quadruple pom-pom in place of the third 5.25-inch gun turret, with its own director. This modification was subsequently extended to most of the original *Didos*, although two of them, *Scylla* and *Charybdis*, were completed in 1941-42 with eight twin 4.5-inch guns because of a shortage of 5.25-inch guns. HMS *Charybdis* was lost in 1943 and her sister suffered serious damage at Normandy in 1944 and so never received her designed armament. Although known as the 'Toothless Terrors' they were in fact good AA ships, with two high-angle directors and radar control.

The two outstanding close-range anti-aircraft weapons were the Swiss 20mm Oerlikon and the Swedish 40mm Bofors, and they steadily ousted older guns in both the US and Royal Navies. Not until the Kamikaze attacks off Okinawa was faith in the Bofors' stopping power shaken, and the US Navy immediately began development of a powerful twin 3-inch (76-mm) automatic mounting. The purpose of increasing the calibre was not only to increase the bursting charge of the shell but also to enable a variable time or proximity fuze to be used. The 3-inch 50 calibre took some time to develop and was not seen until the 17,000-ton *Des Moines* Class commissioned in 1948-49; they also formed the secondary armament of the *Worcester* Class AA cruisers of the same vintage.

Surprisingly few of the ex-enemy cruisers found their way into other hands after 1945. The *Prinz Eugen* was the only German cruiser still afloat in May 1945 and she was taken over by the United States for trials, culminating in the Bikini atom-bomb tests in June 1946. The radioactive hulk was finally scuttled at Kwajalein the following year. The majority of Italian cruisers had been scuttled at the time of the Armistice in 1943 or seized by the Germans, and only 10 survived subsequent bombing or attack by Italian crews manning 'human torpedoes' under British control. Of these the magnificently named *Emanuele Filiberto Duca d'Aosta* was given to Soviet Russia under the peace treaty, while *Eugenio di Savoia* was given to Greece and named *Helli* to commemorate the old cruiser treacherously torpedoed in 1941 to provoke a *casus belli*. In addition France was granted two small cruisers, the *Attilio Regolo* and *Scipione Africano*, for conversion to destroyer leaders.

These small 'sports model' cruisers were among the most unusual cruisers of World War II. Worried by the French *contre-torpilleurs*, the Italian Navy had decided as far back as 1937 to build a new class of 'ocean scouts' or *esploratori oceanici* displacing 3400 tons and capable of 41 knots. Armour inevitably was to be minimal but unlike the French ships these were given a cruiser-armament of four twin 135mm (5.3-inch), six 65mm AA guns and eight torpedo tubes. Weight proved a problem and plans for an aircraft and catapult were dropped. Twelve ships were planned and as they were named after the Roman soldiers and statesmen so dear to Mussolini's heart they became the *Capitani Romani* Class. The hull form was unusual, a flush deck with a transom stern and two

Right: *The somewhat battered looking* USS Tucson *returns from the War in 1945, with bedding hung out to air on the guard rails.*

Below right: *The German cruiser* Prinz Eugen *flying the Stars and Stripes after being taken over by the US Navy in Copenhagen in May 1945. She was used as a nuclear target at Kwajalein Atoll in November 1947.*

The light cruiser Köln *was bombed by US Eighth Air Force planes on 30 March 1945 and sank in Wilhelmshaven. The aircraft and catapult between the funnels had been removed previously and several light AA guns had been added.*

Above: *The Italian light cruiser* Attilio Regolo *in 1942. She and her sister* Scipione Africano *became the French* Chateaurenault *and* Guichen.

widely spaced upright funnels. All reached the designed speed of 41 knots on trials and even with extra fuel and other wartime loadings they proved capable of getting near this in service. They fell victim to the disasters which overtook the Italian war effort, however, and with the bombing of shipyards and worsening shortages of materials only five were completed by September 1943. Two more wartime cruisers ended by being scuttled, two 6000-ton AA cruisers converted from light cruisers ordered by Thailand in 1938 as the *Taksin* and *Naresuan*. The renamed *Etna* and *Vesuvio* would have had three twin 135mm mountings similar to those in the *Capitani Romani* Class and were intended to act as fast transports in addition to their role as fleet escorts.

The French Navy rebuilt its two light cruisers as anti-submarine hunter-killer ships, using ex-German 10.5cm flak mountings as the main armament forward and aft, and Bofors 57mm guns for close-range AA defence. The anti-submarine armament was confined to four sets of triple torpedo tubes for launching short-range homing torpedoes. As the *Chateaurenault* and *Guichen* they lasted until 1961–62, by which time new construction was available. Inspired by this example the reconstituted Italian Navy converted the hulked *Pompeo Magno* and *Giulio Germanico* into

Left: *British officers inspecting the camouflaged hulk of the* Admiral Hipper *in a flooded dock at Kiel. She was subsequently loaded with scrap U-Boat components and scuttled in Heikendorfer Bight.*

cacciatorpediniere conduttori (destroyer leaders) with American-pattern twin 5-inch, 40mm dual-purpose guns and a new Italian-designed triple anti-submarine mortar. In honour of the old armoured cruisers and to forget the Imperial Roman fantasies of the Fascists they were renamed *San Giorgio* and *San Marco* when they rejoined the fleet in 1955. The *San Marco* has since been scrapped but the *San Giorgio* has been rebuilt twice as a training ship, with new machinery and radars, and is expected to continue into the 1980s, a remarkable testimony to the soundness of her design. She still retains the sleek look of the original design but internally she has been transformed, with gas turbines and diesels in place of the original steam turbines.

Although Sweden had traditionally favoured a coast defence navy, with small armoured ships and destroyers or torpedo boats, her navy had also produced some interesting cruiser designs. The *Gotland*, for example, was years ahead of her time in having the ability to operate 11 floatplanes as well as an armament of 6-inch guns. In 1943–44 the flight deck which occupied the after part of the ship was converted into a platform for four twin 40mm AA mountings; anti-aircraft fire was more valuable in the defence of the fleet than her obsolescent floatplanes. In 1943 two 8000-ton light cruisers were ordered, the *Gota Lejon* and *Tre Kroner* to strengthen the Royal Swedish Navy against any possible incursions from the belligerents. When they were finally completed in 1947 they were the finest of their type afloat, fast at 33 knots and well armed with seven 6-inch guns. Although Sweden remained strictly neutral her designers kept abreast of developments in other navies and the two ships had the latest British radars and good fire control.

The main armament of these ships was in a peculiar arrangement with a triple turret and two twin turrets aft. This might well have been three triples had it not been for the fact that a total of two triple and four twin 15cm turrets were available in 1940. These had been ordered in 1937 for two Dutch cruisers from the Swedish armament firm AB Bofors, four triple and four twin mountings. When the Netherlands was overrun by the German Army in 1940 the contract lapsed, but Bofors had already completed most of the work on two of the triples and all the twins. It therefore made sense to design the new Swedish cruisers around these mountings to save both time and money.

This was not the end of the story as far as the Dutch were concerned, and work restarted on the two cruisers after the liberation of the Netherlands. They had narrowly escaped destruction by the Germans in 1944 but were not in bad condition; the *Eendracht* was still on the stocks at Rotterdam but *De Zeven Provincien* had been launched in December at Schiedam. There was no question of completing them to the original design for not only had ideas of cruiser design changed dramatically since 1939 but also much of the equipment originally specified for the two ships was obsolescent. Nor could Sweden provide the missing gun mountings, for the order had been cancelled after delivery of the turrets for the *Gota Lejon* and *Tre Kroner*.

Redesigning the two cruisers would be a massive task for the Netherlands Corps of Constructors and while the Corps was being re-established considerable technical assistance had to be supplied by the British. A new contract

was negotiated with Bofors and it was decided to opt for new twin 6-inch turrets, in the classic disposition of two mountings forward and two aft. This reduced topweight and simplified maintenance, and as an added advantage the mounting had a rate of fire of 15 rounds per minute and elevated to 60 degrees. The original propulsion system was to have been three-shaft turbines driven from six boilers grouped together with a single funnel, but the British strongly recommended the 'unit' system which they had used since the *Amphion* Class in

the early 1930s. The new two-shaft turbines and their four boilers were thus divided into two groups, lessening the risk of a total loss of power from a single torpedo hit amidships. This meant a change to two funnels widely separated, for the same reasons the generators were provided with shock-proof mountings and were more widely distributed.

The anti-aircraft armament was also strengthened, the six twin 40mm mountings being replaced by four twin 57mm enclosed mountings, each with its own

Below: This 1953 view of the Rochester *shows the typical features of the last generation of American heavy cruisers; pole masts, twin 5-inch 38-calibre AA guns, and ten twin 3-inch 50-calibre light AA guns.*

Above: *The heavy cruiser* Rochester *en route for Saigon in February 1954. She and her two sisters of the* Oregon City Class *were modified editions of the* Baltimore *design, with a single funnel to improve arcs of fire for the AA guns.*

Above left: *The USS* Roanoke *and her sister* Worcester *were the ultimate light cruisers, with six twin 6-inch automatic mountings capable of use against aircraft.*

Below: *In 1944 the Swedish* Gotland *was re-armed as an anti-aircraft cruiser to meet the threat of air attack.*

fire-control director. The disposition reflected American experience as much as British; one forward superfiring over the two 6-inch turrets, another aft, and two amidships. Subsequently eight single 40mm Bofors guns were added, with simple tachometric sights. This all took time and work on the ships' hulls did not restart until 1947. The *Eendracht* was renamed *de Ruyter* to commemorate Karel Doorman's flagship sunk in the Battle of the Java Sea, but at the last minute she exchanged names with her sister.

Both ships commissioned at the end of 1953 but trials showed that the attempt to prevent smoke interference by raking the second funnel sharply back was not a great success. The forward uptake had been incorporated into the rear of the bridge structure quite successfully but fumes from the after funnel affected the sensitive radar antennae on the main-mast and so this had to be repositioned on the forward side of the funnel. They were unique in appearance, with tall graceful funnels and a slender hull. With their tiers of gun turrets they gave an impression of power and elegance.

The French also had new ideas about cruisers. They still had the hull of the light cruiser *De Grasse*, laid down in 1938 but suspended in June 1940. The original design had been an improved edition of the *La Galissonière*, with a single funnel and slightly higher speed. Like the Dutch the French knew that the air threat could not be met by a large ship with a purely surface armament. The first operation was to clear the building slip. The hull was completed to the point where it could be launched in September 1946, giving time for redesign work to begin. It was not possible to start work again until 1951, partly because of discussions about the armament but also because of the dire financial position of the French Government. The ship had an inauspicious start to her new career. In June 1954, only two months before starting her first acceptance trials, the building dock was flooded to allow her to be floated out. To everyone's horror the 617-foot long cruiser started to heel and then settled on the bottom of the dock. A seacock in the bottom of the hull had been left open by mistake and a large compartment was flooded. Repairs took another year, so it was not until August 1955 that she sailed on her trials.

When the *De Grasse* was finally completed in the summer of 1956 she set an entirely new standard for anti-aircraft cruisers, with the whole super-structure covered in guns. There were four twin 5-inch mountings forward, on three levels (two on the centre-line and two winged out on either beam) and a similar disposition aft; in addition there were 10 twin 57mm mountings, five forward and five aft (two on the centre-line and four on either beam). The biggest problem with such a layout was supplying ammunition to such a large number of guns. The 57mm guns in particular, with a rate of fire of 130 rounds per minute, would very quickly use up a normal ready-use allowance. Having the turrets so high on either side

of the superstructure also created problems in positioning the hoists, so the expedient of having some magazines above the waterline was adopted. This involved some risk from battle damage, which other navies might have found unacceptable, but it ensured that the guns would keep firing.

While the *De Grasse* was still completing, the French Navy ordered a second anti-aircraft cruiser, this time built for the purpose. The *Colbert* had an almost identical disposition of guns but differed from the *De Grasse* in the arrangement of her armour. The two ships were distinctive in appearance, with a single fat funnel emphasising the pyramid effect of the small gun mountings around the superstructure. One interesting point about the 5-inch guns is that they were made in France with a purely French mounting but were chambered to take the standard US Navy 5-inch round, to ensure supplies of ammunition in wartime. The 57mm mountings were similarly built in France but under licence from AB Bofors in Sweden.

For the first few years after 1945 the British contented themselves with modernising the *Southampton* and *Fiji* Classes. This consisted of providing air-conditioning for ships serving in the tropics, updating the radar and standardising the close-range AA armament. Late in World War II the bigger cruisers lost one of their after gun turrets (always the superimposed 'X' mounting) to allow space for additional AA guns. Initially these were the standard four-barrelled pom-poms but as soon as mountings became available twin 40mm Bofors guns replaced them. After the war this process continued, with single Bofors guns replacing single and twin 20mm guns. Many were given a variant of the American Mark 63 radar-control for their twin 4-inch AA guns.

Some idea of the transformation of British cruisers' armament can be gauged by what happened to HMS *Belfast*. This ship, originally a sister to the ill-fated *Edinburgh*, had been mined in the very first weeks of war on 21 November 1939. As the first major victim of the new magnetic mine she provided valuable but expensive lessons. The ship actually broke her back, the main girder fractured and cracks reached right up to the weather deck amidships. Under normal circumstances she would have been beyond repair but the Royal Navy could not afford to write off a brand-new

Centre: Colbert *commissioned in 1959 and had an unusual armament of eight twin 5-inch and ten twin 57mm guns.*

Above: *The* Tre Kroner *is seen here on trials in 1947. She utilised 6-inch mountings ordered pre-war.*

Left: *The old training cruiser Jeanne d'Arc passing under the rebuilt high-level bridge in Brest Arsenal. After a distinguished career spanning over 30 years she was replaced by a new ship of the same name in 1964.*

Below: *The imposing Mark 26 twin automatic 6-inch turret and broad bridge front of HMS Blake, completed in 1961. She and her two sisters were suspended from 1946 to 1955 and then completed to a radically different design.*

DANGER
TURRET MAY
MOVE WITHOUT
WARNING

11,550-ton cruiser, so she was rebuilt over a period of three years. Wartime shortages played their part, but even without all the wartime problems she needed a major piece of ship-surgery. A massive 'bulge' ran over two-thirds of her length to strengthen the hull. This also had the effect of permitting much more topweight than the original designers had envisaged.

Her original close-range armament had been two eight-barrelled pom-poms and two quadruple 0.5-inch machine guns, but when she rejoined the Home Fleet at the end of 1942 she had five twin 20mm and eight single 20mm Oerlikons in place of the machine guns. When she went out to the Pacific in May 1945 she was given four more quadruple pom-poms, seven more twin 20mm guns and two singles in place of the original eight. When she arrived in Sydney the threat of kamikaze attack caused the dockyard there to give her four single pom-poms and five 40mm Bofors guns, in place of five twin 20mm, and an extra pair of 20mm singles. By the time of the Korean War the close-range armament had been reduced to the six multiple pom-poms and only nine 40mm Bofors guns.

The *Belfast* was given a further modernisation in 1956–59, this time she emerged with a new bridge, lattice masts in place of the tripods and a much improved close-range armament. The 4-inch guns were retained but twin 40mm Mark 5 mountings replaced the motley collection of pom-poms and single Bofors guns. More important, each group of AA guns had its own director, one on either side of the bridge controlling the forward group of four 40mm mountings, two amidships controlling the 4-inch guns and another two controlling after 40mm guns.

Three incomplete cruisers of a modified *Fiji* design, the *Tiger* Class, had been laid up in 1946 to allow time for redesign and in 1954 it was announced that they would be completed to a radically new design. The intention was to give them a combined surface and anti-aircraft capability, so instead of following the French idea of scores of light guns they were given a dual-purpose 6-inch gun mounting for the main armament, backed up by a powerful 3-inch AA mounting.

Both of these developments owed much to American thinking. The 6-inch Mark 26 was the approximate equivalent of the dual-purpose mountings in the USS *Worcester*, and the 3-inch 70-calibre twin automatic was a development of an improved version of the 3-inch 50 calibre rushed into production after the devastation caused by kamikaze attacks in 1945. However the weight of a fully automatic twin 6-inch was 156 tons and on a standard displacement intended to be only 8800 tons there was

Below: *Painting the* Gloire. *Note the twin 21.7-inch torpedo tubes.*

Left: *Looking aft along the starboard side of HMS* Blake *on her completion in 1961.*

Below: *HMS* Superb *was completed at the end of 1945.*

Below: *The reconstructed* Oklahoma City. *The Talos guided missiles provided vital air defence at over 60 miles range. miles.*

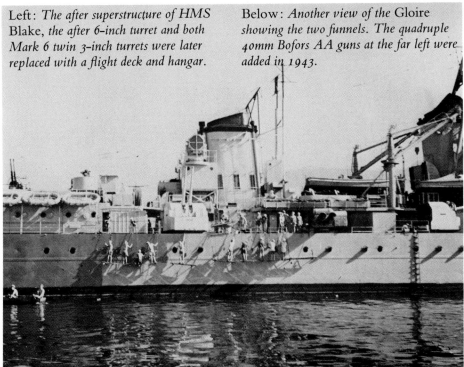

Left: *The after superstructure of HMS* Blake, *the after 6-inch turret and both Mark 6 twin 3-inch turrets were later replaced with a flight deck and hangar.*

Below: *Another view of the* Gloire *showing the two funnels. The quadruple 40mm Bofors AA guns at the far left were added in 1943.*

no question of mounting more than two turrets, and only three of the 3-inch Mark 6 mountings. As with the French AA cruisers there was also the knotty problem of how to provide enough ammunition; the 6-inch fired 20-25 rounds per minute and the 3-inch could fire 120 rounds. However the RN could not afford to be choosy. Its older cruisers had seen very arduous wartime service and were so worn out that they were not worth the cost of reconstruction.

The *Didos* were too small to warrant modernisation, although an exception was made for New Zealand in 1955-56 when the *Royalist* was completely rebuilt. She was given new masts, a new bridge, modern fire control and the original close-range armament was replaced by three automatic 40mm mountings and three singles. By 1958 there were only 13 of the various *Southampton* and *Fiji* Class variants, excluding the three *Tigers* still under conversion, and it was fairly obvious that they had little value in modern warfare.

The United States' Navy, as might be expected, had an embarrassingly large number of cruisers. To add to the problems of maintaining so many ships in anything like a good state of repair in the 'mothball fleet', the nine worn-out prewar heavy cruisers of the *Northampton*, *San Francisco* and *Wichita* Classes which had been struck off after 1945 had to be re-instated in 1952 to appease public opinion. There were 57 assorted gunarmed cruisers still nominally effective in 1958. However, like everyone else, the US Navy was aware that the concept of the cruiser was changing. The utility of this vast array of ships, most of them lacking modern radars and fire control, was questionable.

In 1948 an interesting experimental light cruiser was laid down. The USS *Norfolk* (CLK. 1) was intended to be a large, weatherly anti-submarine ship to enable her to hunt and destroy submarines on the high seas regardless of bad weather. Although her hull was that of a light cruiser, displacing nearly 6000 tons standard, her role overlapped that of the big destroyer and she was eventually reclassified as a destroyer leader (DL). She undoubtedly provided the inspiration for the French and Italian conversions of the *Capitani Romani* hulls.

As part of the search to find an answer to the kamikaze attacks the US Navy had initiated the 'Bumblebee' programme as early as 1944, to develop a guided weapon capable of destroying high-speed aircraft. After a decade of development the result, the Terrier guided missile, was fired for the first time from the old battleship *Mississippi*. Terrier was a big weapon 27-foot long and weighing more than a 16-inch shell without its associated fire control and radar, so there was little point in trying to install it in small warships. The logical ship to take Terrier to sea was a big cruiser and so in 1954 the two *Baltimore* Class, *Boston* and *Canberra*, were taken in hand for reconstruction. When they reappeared in 1955-56 they were re-numbered CAG. 1 and CAG. 2, the world's first guided-missile cruisers.

The profile was completely altered, for the reconstruction had followed the lines of the single-funnelled *Oregon City* Class in order to make room for the new equipment. The entire after super-structure and the 143-ton triple turret were replaced by platforms carrying two twin-arm launchers, two directors on tall pedestals and a big platform for new radars. Below decks the former shell-rooms and powder magazines were re-placed by mechanical stowage and load-ing gear for a total of 144 Terrier missiles, stored and loaded vertically. This degree of mechanisation was needed to handle such big weapons. Two missiles could be launched every 30 seconds. Terrier was a beam-riding missile, homing onto hostile aircraft by following a radar beam generated by the fire-control director.

The success of this conversion led to six of the *Cleveland* Class being con-verted in 1956-60. The *Providence*, *Springfield* and *Topeka* were given one twin-arm Terrier launcher and two directors aft (it had been found that the firing rate of one launcher was more than adequate to cope with the capacity of the guidance system) but the *Galves-ton*, *Little Rock* and *Oklahoma City* were given the longer-range Talos missile. The difference in size of the Talos meant that only 46 could be carried as against 120 Terriers. Unlike the *Boston* and *Canberra*, the *Clevelands* retained their two slim funnels but were given two very tall lattice masts to carry the radar arrays. Two of the ships retained both triple 6-inch turrets and the twin 5-inch forward but the *Little Rock*, *Oklahoma City*, *Providence* and *Spring-field* were fitted as Fleet Flagships, and to provide the extra space needed they had only one 6-inch turret. They were given the new designation CLG. 3-8 to

Below and right: Two views of the Italian helicopter cruiser Vittorio Veneto. *She has a twin surface-to-air missile launcher forward and a hangar and flight deck aft for operating light AB-20 anti-submarine helicopters.*

distinguish them from the 'heavy' conversions, although the difference in gun calibre had little to do with their relative effectiveness.

The success of these conversions led to a further programme of conversion starting in fiscal year 1958. This was at a time when the US Navy had studied a whole range of projects for missile ships, including the *Iowa* Class battleships. Although these were ruled out as being too costly, what was authorised turned out to be as expensive at $170 million. Three of the heavy cruisers were earmarked, the single-funnelled *Oregon City* and the two-funnelled *Chicago* and *Fall River*. The *Albany* was substituted for the *Oregon City* because she was in better condition, and finally the *Columbus* was substituted for the *Fall River*. The three conversions were to be reclassified as CG. 10-12.

The conversion was much more elaborate than anything previously envisaged. The hull was stripped down to the weather deck and an entirely new superstructure was built up, comprising two lofty 'macks' or combined 'mast-and stack' with a high narrow bridge. There were twin-arm Talos missile launchers forward and aft and Tartar missile launchers on either side of the

bridge. This gave superb all-round coverage, with the 70-mile Talos for long-range defence and the shorter-range Tartar to deal with targets which got through the outer screen. In addition there was an eight-cell launcher amidships for Asroc anti-submarine missiles and provision internally for eight Polaris ballistic missiles, to allow for any future decision to deploy the nuclear deterrent in surface ships. Originally no guns of any sort were provided but after they had recommissioned fears of attack by North Vietnamese surface craft led to the installation of two obsolescent 5-inch guns in open mountings, one on either side of the after 'mack' to provide some sort of basic defence.

Known as the 'tall ladies' because of their high profiles the three ships saw considerable active service after completing their reconstructions in 1963-64. Their comprehensive aircraft-direction facilities were tested during the Vietnam War. It is recorded that one controller directing fighters in the *Chicago* assisted in shooting down 21 MiGs. In 1972 she covered the minelaying operation off Haiphong. When North Vietnamese interceptors were picked up on radar moving towards the minelaying aircraft, the cruiser's Talos missiles were able to shoot down one MiG at a range of 48 miles and turn the rest away. Another use for Talos was with an anti-radiation homing head, allowing them to destroy radar sites in North Vietnam before air-strikes. There is a limit to the amount of 'stretch' left in hulls which were launched as long ago as 1944-45, added to which is the rising cost of manning ships with an elderly steam plant. In August 1976 the *Columbus* (CG. 12) was struck off the effective list and it is only a matter of time before her two sisters go the same way.

By 1968 the original conversions, *Boston* and *Canberra*, were considered unsuitable for the task of defending the Fleet against air attack because of the obsolescence of the BW-1 Terrier missile systems. Paradoxically, they proved extremely useful off Vietnam because they had retained their forward triple 8-inch guns. Both they and the unconverted heavy cruisers served on the 'gun-line' in Vietnam, pounding Vietcong and North Vietnamese positions far more effectively than the Navy and Air Force ground attack aircraft. The virtue of naval bombardment has always been that it can be sustained for as long as ammunition lasts, and its methodical and repetitive nature has a worse effect on enemy morale than occasional air strikes, however devastating they may be.

The advantage of converting cruisers to guided-missile ships was exactly the same as it had always been; their endurance gave them greater mobility than smaller ships such as destroyers and their size meant that they could carry a worthwhile number of missiles. Once the US Navy had shown the way others followed suit. The Royal Netherlands Navy rebuilt the *De Zeven Provincien* on similar lines, with a twin Terrier launcher and fire control in place of the after turret, while the Italians did a similar job on the rather old light cruiser *Giuseppe Garibaldi*.

The Italians took matters a step further, and in 1958 laid down a pair of *incrociatori di scorta* or escort cruisers armed with Terriers. The *Andrea Doria* and *Caio Duilio* set an entirely new standard, with a gun-armament of only eight single 3-inch guns, a twin-armed Terrier launcher forward and a big flight deck and hangar aft for handling four small anti-submarine helicopters. All this and a speed of 30 knots was achieved on a full load of 6500 tons. They proved to be on the small side for such a heavy load of

Far left: Giuseppe Garibaldi *was converted to a missile cruiser in 1957-62.*

Left: *HMS* Blake *shadowing a Soviet frigate after her 1965-69 conversion.*

weaponry, however, and the concept was expanded to the 8500-ton *Vittorio Veneto* built in 1965-69. As before, the Terrier launcher was forward and gun-armament was restricted to four 3-inch automatic AA guns on either side amidships, but nine Agusta-Bell helicopters could be accommodated aft.

Having spent a large amount of money completing the three *Tiger* Class in 1959-61 the British were not likely to consider a missile conversion for them. In any case their hulls were too small to allow the British Seaslug or Sea Dart missiles to be installed. There was an urgent need to get more anti-submarine helicopters to sea, and with the Italian example to inspire them the Royal Navy in 1964 sanctioned a conversion which replaced the after 6-inch turret with a flight deck and hangar. The result is two of the ugliest ships afloat (the *Lion* was never converted) with a huge boxlike hangar and an ungainly flight deck overhanging the narrow transom stern. To cope with the increase in topweight the midships 3-inch AA guns had to be removed but the directors were retained to provide tracking for the quadruple Seacat short-range missiles which replaced the guns. The *Blake* and *Tiger* have ended up with two different calibres of gun, both forward of the bridge, but there is such a lack of medium-calibre guns for shore bombardment that this oddity had to be tolerated. On a slightly greater tonnage than the Italian *Vittorio Veneto* only four helicopters are carried, but these are the much bigger Sea King type.

All these conversions of World War II cruisers suffered from the inherent problems of pressing new wine into old bottles. However it wrang a few more years service out of ships which might otherwise have gone to the scrapyard, and showed that the cruiser could adapt to modern warfare. In the 1950s it had been fashionable to predict that the cruiser would soon follow the battleship into obsolescence. Nobody made such a suggestion after seeing the exceptional performance of the missile cruisers in the Vietnam War.

Left: *HMS* Tiger *in 1977 showing the hangar and flight deck aft.*

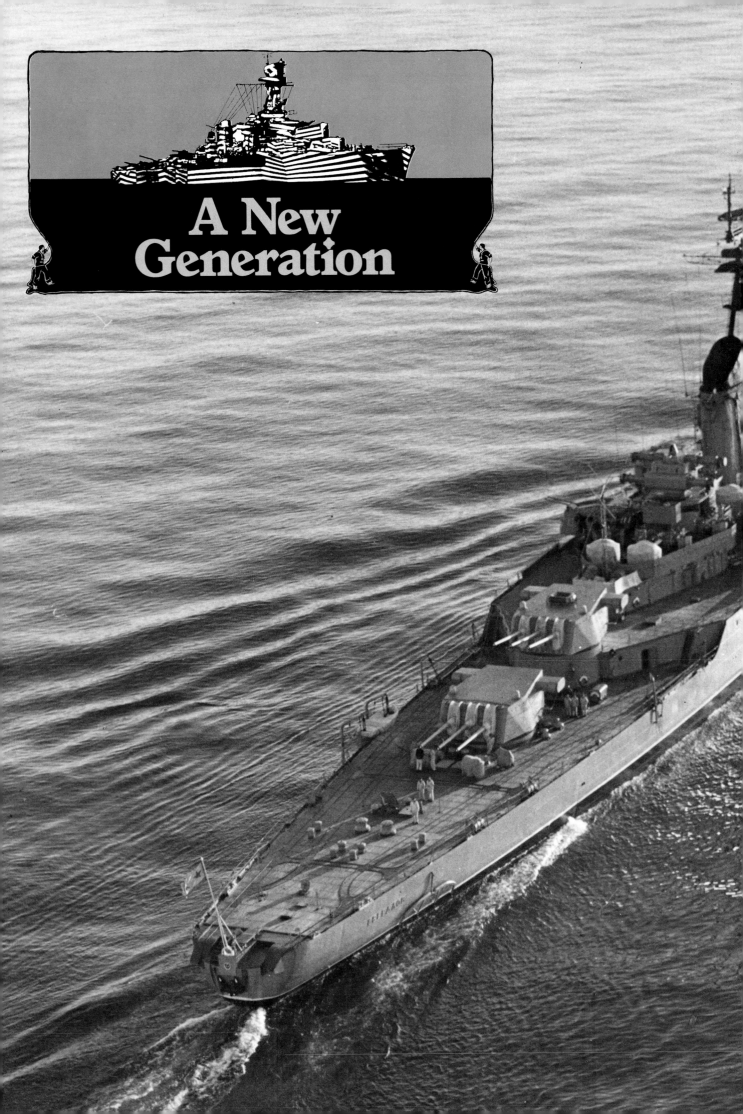

A New
Generation

The severely classical lines of the Soviet Sverdlov betray the Italian origin of her design.

Although most navies gave up the idea of the big gun-armed cruiser after World War II there was one exception. The Soviet Union had been expanding its navy before the German invasion in June 1941 and although much of the new construction had been destroyed either by enemy action, or by the Russians to keep it out of German hands, a number of hulls survived in 1945.

Joseph Stalin had always dreamed of a big navy and his naval commander-in-chief, Admiral Kuznetsov, was given funds to complete five of the *Chapaev* Class. These were improved editions of the pre-war *Kirov* Class, and like them had been designed with Italian technical assistance. However in place of the *Kirovs'* three triple 180mm (7.1-inch) guns the *Chapaevs* were given four triple 150mm (5.9-inch). The Italian influence was particularly noticeable in their appearance; with two widely spaced capped funnels they looked like the *Zara* and *Bolzano* Classes, but the secondary armament and fire control were based on German technology.

While work was being restarted on the *Chapaev* Class a new class of slightly improved and enlarged ships was laid down. This was the handsome *Sverdlov* Class, which had the same main armament as the *Chapaev* and the same layout. The *Chapaev* Class did not attract a great deal of comment in the West but in 1952 the *Sverdlov* was sent to Britain to represent the Soviet Union at Queen Elizabeth's Coronation Naval Review. There her elegant lines and immaculate handling made a big impression. Speculation was rife about her capabilities, and her essentially old-fashioned features were overlooked. She was credited with very high speed, outstanding man-oeuvrability and very heavy protection. Although she was very little bigger than the 11,300-ton *Chapaev* she was officially credited with being 4000 tons heavier. Looked at today her optical range-finding equipment and low-angle main armament stamp her as a pre-war design. It is doubtful if she would have made much of an impression against Western navies, but in the 1950s it was fashionable in naval circles to talk luridly of the '*Sverdlov* cruiser-threat'. Ludicrous as it may sound, one of the arguments for retaining battleships in the USN and RN was their value against the *Sverdlovs* and the British went so far as to design a '*Sverdlov*-killing' destroyer, armed with rapid-fire 5-inch guns and steaming at 38 knots.

In all 24 *Sverdlov*s were planned and 20 keels were laid but after the death of Stalin and the retirement of Kuznetsov a mood of reaction set in. Nikita Kruschev admitted as much when he told the West that he was scrapping all his cruisers and recommended them to do the same. As with other Russian pronouncements this was not quite what happened, and only six incomplete hulls were scrapped. Two were subsequently transferred to Indonesia, one was scrapped in 1969 and the others serve in variety of subsidiary roles. Unlike other navies' cruisers they were not given a massive reconstruction, although three, the *Dzerzhinski*, *Admiral Senyavin* and *Zhdanov* were given experimental guided-missile installations.

The last *Sverdlov* commissioned in 1956, but only a year later an entirely new type of ship was laid down, the *raketny kreiser* or 'rocket cruiser'. Known to the West under the code-name *Kynda* but actually called the *Grozny* Class, four were laid down in 1957-61 and completed between 1961 and 1965. It is possible that as many as 12 were planned, but with eight very large missile tubes on deck, reloads in the superstructure, a surface-to-air missile launcher and a massive array of radars it is almost certain that severe stability problems were encountered, so the programme stopped at four ships. To Western observers the massive surface-to-surface missiles, code-named SS-N-1 or *Shaddock*, with its range of 170 miles gave the Soviet Navy a big advantage over Western ships. Immediately they were seen to be successors to the *Sverdlov*, roaming the oceans and hunting down American aircraft carriers. The provision of double guidance radars for both surface and anti-aircraft missile systems was cited as proof of Soviet designers' wisdom in allowing for battle damage.

A closer look at the *Kynda* raises some

doubts about the role assumed for them by most Western commentators. For one thing the 170-mile range for the SS-N-1 missiles could only be achieved if the missile is given mid-course guidance, and as the *Kynda* design does not include a helicopter it must be assumed that she was intended to operate mainly in waters dominated by Russian air power – not the world's oceans. This limitation is confirmed by the lack of a high-performance search radar, and the much-praised doubling up of fire-control radars now seems to be a reflection of their lack of reliability, not a doubling of efficiency. Another interesting point is that although the *Grozny*, *Varyag*, *Admiral Golovko* and *Admiral Fokin* were all built at the Zhdanov yard in Leningrad and operated with the Northern Fleet they were subsequently modified to reduce topweight and then sent to the less demanding Pacific and Black Sea Fleets. However, as the vanguard of an entirely new concept of missile-armed ships the *Kynda* Class deserve an important place in cruiser history.

Above: *The* Sverdlov *and the shadowing* Blake.

During the 1950s and 1960s the major Western navies occupied themselves with converting cruisers to launch missiles, but there was a tacit assumption that the day of the cruiser as a separate category was over. To many observers the only justification for all the cruiser conversions was their capacity to take the bulky first generation surface-to-air missiles such as Terrier and Talos.

Below: *The French* Suffren *represents a smaller type of conventionally powered missile cruiser. The 'golfball' is a cover for a big 3-D radar and the Masurca missile guidance radars can be seen aft.*

All this changed in 1957 when the United States' Navy laid the keel of a 14,000-ton nuclear-powered cruiser (CLGN-160, later redesignated CGN-160 and finally CG-9) to be called *Long Beach*. Not only was she the first cruiser to be built since 1945 but also the world's first nuclear-powered surface warship and the first to be armed with nothing but guided missiles. She set entirely new standards in cruiser design, with no armour protection to the hull, although some deck-plating was provided over the magazines. The planned displacement was to have been 7800 tons but by the time the order was placed in 1956 this had risen to 11,000 tons after a second Terrier missile system was added. A subsequent decision to add the long-range Talos aft (both Terrier systems were forward) pushed standard displacement up to 14,200 tons. Although this was less than the *Des Moines* Class the absence of armour resulted in a hull 21 feet longer and drawing over 4 feet more water.

Top: *The USS* Nimitz *and the cruisers* California *and* South Carolina *at Norfolk Navy Yard, make up the most powerful surface force in the world.*

Above: *The nuclear cruiser* Virginia *looks under-armed by comparison with earlier cruisers but is far more potent than any previous generation of warships.*

Having two Westinghouse pressurised-water cooled reactors to provide steam for the two turbines meant that uptakes and funnels were dispensed with, and for the first time designers could lay out the superstructure to suit themselves. The result was a big square block of bridgework with unique 'bill-board' radar arrays on the outer faces, free from corrosive funnel gases and sited for maximum efficiency. Although the speed of 30 knots was slightly more modest than earlier cruisers it was constantly available and so the *Long Beach* would be an ideal escort for big carriers. In fact after she was completed in 1961 she operated with the nuclear-powered attack carrier *Enterprise* and it was soon realised that conventionally powered escorts were simply not suited to the task as they used so much fuel in the high-speed steaming required to keep up with the *Enterprise*.

The C1W reactors were similar to the A2W type in the *Enterprise* but in the year that the *Long Beach* was laid down, work started on a prototype reactor small enough to be installed in a 'destroyer-sized' ship. This meant a displacement of about the same as the original figure planned for the *Long Beach*, which was achieved. In 1959 the keel of the first nuclear-powered DLG or frigate was laid. The *Bainbridge* (DLGN-25) displaced 7600 tons and differed from the *Long Beach* principally

in having her two Terrier missile systems at either end of the ship, and no Talos. Another difference was that she had a more conventional layout of superstructure, with rotating radar scanners on a tall lattice mast instead of the 'billboards'.

The commissioning of the *Bainbridge* in 1962 gave the US Navy the world's first nuclear task force with the *Enterprise* and *Long Beach*, and there was talk of an all-nuclear navy. But the cost was staggering, $332.85 million for the *Long Beach* and $163.2 million for the *Bainbridge*. Congress recoiled from the implications of going all-nuclear; fewer ships and the need for much more highly qualified engineers than ever before. Fiscal Year 1958 therefore included money for three 'fossil-fuelled' frigates, and six more were authorised the following year.

Many lessons were learned from previous conversions. Like the bigger ships these 5600-tonners were made 'double-enders' with Terrier missile systems forward and aft. The superstructure was modelled on the *Bainbridge* but the uptakes from the boilers were in 'macks' as in the heavy cruiser conversions. They were completed in 1962-64, and in common with other US Navy ships were given a token gun armament for dealing with small surface targets, two twin 3-inch 50-calibre mountings amidships. The *Leahy* Class (DLG. 16-24)

proved very successful and in 1962-67 a further nine of improved design were ordered. The *Belknap* Class (DLG. 26-34) was nearly 1000 tons bigger but reverted to having only one missile system forward. The reason for this apparently retrograde step was to allow for a bigger missile magazine in the forepart of the hull and to leave room for a 5-inch dual-purpose gun and helicopter hangar aft. The *Leahy* Class had carried an 8-cell Asroc missile launcher for anti-submarine defence but the *Belknaps* were given a combined Terrier/Asroc launcher that was served from a common magazine.

Both classes have since benefited from improvements in missile technology, with Terrier replaced by the lighter and more effective Standard missile in its ER (extended range) form. The provision of a helicopter hangar in the *Belknap* Class proved a limited blessing for it had been intended for a pair of DASH drone anti-submarine helicopters. The expensive failure of the DASH programme in the mid-1960s left them without a helicopter, but when a new interim light shipboard helicopter became available

the flight deck and hangar provided for DASH proved unsuitable. Not until 1971 was the *Belknap* modified to allow her to operate the first SH-2D Light Airborne Multi-Purpose System (LAMPS) helicopter.

There was a return to nuclear power in 1962 when DLGN-35 was authorised, later to commission in 1967 as the *Truxtun*. Although basically an improved edition of the *Bainbridge* on a slightly greater tonnage she was in effect a nuclear edition of the *Belknap* Class, but with the 5-inch gun forward and the Terrier missiles aft. The reason for this change of policy was that Congress had authorised seven frigates in Fiscal Year 1962 (DLG. 29-35) but then stipulated that the seventh ship must be nuclear. All 20 frigates were reclassified as cruisers on 30 June 1975, although 10 earlier frigates of similar fighting power to the *Leahy* Class were downgraded to destroyers. The change, although confusing at the time, was entirely logical for these fast carrier escorts were the logical successors of the old sailing frigates and could therefore be reasonably termed cruisers.

The British were not only unable to afford nuclear cruisers but also suffered from economising politicians and a Treasury which questioned the need for cruisers at all. As a result their first

Above: *The Soviet* Kara *Class missile-cruiser* Kerch *photographed in the Mediterranean in 1976.*

Below: *The Soviet* Kresta II *Class* Admiral Makarov *shadowing the British carrier* Ark Royal *during a NATO exercise in September 1978.*

guided-missile ships had to be disguised as destroyers to get financial approval, and have ever since been rated as DLGs. At 5440 tons standard and with traditional 'County' cruiser names they bear no resemblance to any destroyers past or present, apart from the fact that they are unarmoured (like the US Navy's and other DLGs), and should be rated as light cruisers. The first two ships, *Devonshire* and *Hampshire* were laid down in 1959, followed by *London* and *Kent* in 1960. Between 1962 and 1966 four more were ordered, the *Devonshire* entered service in 1962 and the last ships *Antrim* and *Norfolk* were commissioned in 1970.

The origins of the design lay in the '*Sverdlov*-killer' projected in the early 1950s but cancelled because it had nothing but three dual-purpose 5-inch guns with which to defend itself against aircraft. It is said that the new First Sea Lord, Admiral of the Fleet Earl Mountbatten, said on seeing the sketch designs that he would not dare to build a ship of such size without a guided-missile system for defence against aircraft. The very different requirements for accommodating the Royal Navy's contemporary surface-to-air missile, the Seaslug, meant that the ship had to be totally redesigned, and finally little was left but the machinery. Seaslug was a beam-riding missile like the US Navy's Terrier

but because its booster motors were clustered around the body of the missile it was much bulkier than the Terrier, and so the vertical loading system of the *Boston* and *Canberra* could not be considered. Instead the missile was stowed horizontally well forward in the ship and brought up on a hoist to quarterdeck level. It then travelled aft through a tunnel inside the ship and was loaded horizontally onto a twin launcher right aft. The small number of missiles carried (believed to be as few as 14, although 36 has been claimed) would not have been so bad had Seaslug been a very good missile but its guidance system was not particularly efficient. The missile itself was reliable, however, and the Mark 2 version fitted in the later ships, *Antrim*, *Glamorgan*, *Fife* and *Norfolk* is credited with a limited surface-to-surface capability. However the 'Counties' were undoubtedly handsome and weatherly ships, with good freeboard and two balanced low funnels. British designers did not favour the mack as they preferred to use wind flow to carry smoke clear of radar antennae and aerials. In this respect time has shown that the technical problems of macks outweighed their usefulness.

The most interesting feature of the 'Counties' was their machinery. The problems with steam machinery had always been the time taken to build up

a head of steam and the need to lay up a ship for six months or more if machinery repairs were needed. In the mid-1950s the reigning obsession was the 'Four Minute Warning', four minutes being the time between the launching of an intercontinental ballistic missile (ICBM) and its arrival on target. As naval bases were inevitably among the most likely targets for ICBMs any improvement in the ability of ships to leave harbour was welcomed, and the British looked at ways of adapting the aircraft turbo-jet to naval use. Several smaller British warships had run trials with gas turbine propulsion, but the 'County' Class were the first large warships to have them. Two G6 gas turbines provided boost power, while on the same shafts two steam turbines provided cruising and main power. This meant that the ships could leave harbour on gas turbines alone and could also use their power to boost top speed.

The 'Counties' also introduced the helicopter as an integral part of the design. They carried a Wessex anti-submarine helicopter in a hangar on the port side aft. Forward they carried a conventional gun armament, two twin 4.5-inch dual-purpose guns, but on either side aft they were armed with quadruple Seacat short-range surface-to-air missiles. A plan to fit them with torpedo tubes was dropped as the helicopter provided a better means of delivery. In 1972–74 the *Norfolk* lost one 4.5-inch mounting and received four of the French Exocet surface-to-surface missiles to improve her surface strike capability, and since then three of her sisters have been similarly re-armed.

An improved type of light cruiser/DLG was planned to follow the 'Counties'. Like them the Type 82 'destroyer' was to be a missile-armed fleet escort with Combined Steam And Gas (COSAG) machinery but instead of the cumbersome Seaslug they were to be armed with the new Sea Dart missile which has semi-active radar homing and ramjet propulsion. Four were planned as escorts for a new pair of aircraft carriers (redesignated CVA.01 and CVA.02), but when the aircraft carrier programme was axed in 1966 the four Type 82 ships had no role. Shortly afterwards three were cancelled but the lead ship *Bristol* went ahead as the Royal Navy was desperately short of cruiser-type ships with good command facilities and endurance. The *Bristol* appeared in 1973, but because her intended role had

Below: *Gun-armed cruisers came back when the new warships failed to provide gunfire support in Vietnam. The* Canberra *fires at the North Vietnamese coast in 1967.*

182

Below: *The stern of HMS Bristol, showing her twin Sea Dart missile launcher and the dome covering the Type 909 guidance radar. The after funnels are divided to provide easy access to the twin gas turbines.*

D23

vanished she has always seemed something of a white elephant. However she has excellent command and communications facilities and with her Sea Dart missile system and Ikara anti-submarine missile system she is a potent warship. With the revival of fixed-wing aviation in the RN she will no doubt redeem her reputation.

It is significant that when the Royal Navy finally rescinded the decision to get rid of aircraft carriers the new ship was described as a cruiser. Because a flat deck and a starboard island superstructure would suggest an aircraft carrier to even the most ill-informed observer the new design was labelled a 'through-deck cruiser'. This unhappy term was subsequently changed to 'command cruiser', then to 'anti-submarine' cruiser. It is currently almost sheepishly admitted to be an aircraft carrier, albeit one equipped with vertical take-off Sea Harrier aircraft and helicopters, but the word 'cruiser' still suggests a major unit with high endurance and good command facilities. The first of a class of three such ships, HMS *Invincible*, started her trials in the spring of 1979.

The Soviet Navy, having pioneered the surface-strike cruiser in the *Kynda* Class, decided to rectify the more obvious faults in their next class. Work apparently started on this project in 1964. Code-named *Kresta* by NATO when she first appeared in 1970 the *Vize-Admiral Drozd* looked quite different from her predecessors, with a massive central mack and tall radar tower. The hull form is also different, with a long low upper deck running nearly the whole length of the hull. Instead of the fore-and-aft quadruple missile tubes the *Kresta* carried two pairs, one on either side of the bridge. Although current Western thinking is that no reloads for the SS-N-3 *Shaddock* missiles are carried, there might well be space for four reloads in the forward deckhouse, and the launching tubes are hinged. Two important deficiencies in the *Kynda* design were rectified; a helicopter hangar is provided right aft and the big air-warning radar is sited on the mack. The *Hormone-B* helicopter carried a radar and could provide mid-course guidance for the *Shaddock* missiles.

The appearance of a modified version of the *Kresta* in 1970 complicated the assessment of this new Soviet design. The *Kronstadt* was code-named *Kresta II*, and construction of *Kresta I* terminated after only four ships were built. The main external difference was the redesign of the pyramidal tower amidships to carry new 3-D radar antenna and the replacement of the horizontal missile tubes by missile launchers in quadruple boxes angled up at 20 degrees. For some years this was reputed to be a new surface-to-surface missile, code-named SSN-10, and was credited with horizon range. However it is now believed to be the SS-N-14, an anti-submarine missile with a range of up to 30 miles (although a much lower range is likely). This helps to explain the Soviet designation for the *Kresta II, Bolshoi Protivolodochny Korabl* or Large Anti-submarine ship, but it casts doubt over the ship's ability to defend herself against surface attack or, for that matter, to pose a threat to Western surface ships. After all, the SS-N-3 was credited with as much as 300 miles' range (probably only 170 miles) and the helicopter had been provided for the purpose of mid-course guidance. Apart from the SS-N-14 missile, which is a winged torpedo similar to the Anglo-Australian Ikara and the French Malafon in principle, the only other anti-submarine weapons carried on either type are two pairs of multiple rocket-launchers.

The *Kresta II* is clearly more successful than the *Kresta I* for 10 ships have been completed since 1970, overlapping a later class. However it is believed that the *Admiral Yumashev* will be the last. They have been superseded by the similar but larger (8200 tons) *Kara* type, of which the *Nikolaiev* was the first in 1973. The

Right: *The* Admiral Makarov *puts on a spurt to get ahead of HMS* Ark Royal *during a NATO exercise in 1978.*

Below: *The old cruiser* Jeanne d'Arc *and her replacement,* la Résolue, *in 1964.*

armament of the *Kresta II* has been repeated in roughly the same layout but instead of the rather ugly mack there is a big square funnel. The reason for this is the replacement of steam turbines by gas turbines, whose massive heat output cannot be handled adequately by a mack. Although some Western authorities credit the *Kara* type with massive power and speed these are probably grossly overestimated; on roughly the same dimensions as an American nuclear cruiser capable of 30 knots she is claimed to have double the power and 34 knots.

In mid-1967 the Russians produced their first helicopter carrier, the 14,500-ton *Moskva*. She and her sister *Leningrad* are officially described as *Protivolodochny Kreyser* or anti-submarine cruisers. In general layout they resemble the French *Jeanne d'Arc* in having a centre-line superstructure and conventional guided-missile cruiser bow, but a flight deck aft as if two different ships have been joined together. Unlike the British *Invincible* Class they are obviously not intended to operate anything but helicopters. Clearly the Soviet Navy was providing itself with a more effective anti-submarine arm by taking more ASW helicopters to sea. The reason was the growing awareness of the threat posed by Polaris submarines, particularly in the Mediterranean.

Of even more significance was the next class of 'anti-submarine cruisers', the *Kiev* Class. When she appeared late in 1976 she threw Western observers into a fever of apprehension and speculation for she was clearly intended to operate fixed-wing aircraft, with a starboard island and angled flight deck. The presence of a flight of Yak-36

Below: *The Soviet missile cruiser* Admiral Golovko, *one of four* Kyndas.

Forger VTOL aircraft on her flight deck immediately sparked off fears that the Soviet Navy was going into the aircraft carrier game, taking on the US Navy on the high seas and generally assuming a much greater offensive capacity.

Yet on closer examination the *Kiev* proves to be as much of a hybrid as the *Moskva*, with a heavy battery of eight SS-N-12 surface-to-surface missiles, a surface-to-air missile launcher and a twin 76mm gun mounting on the forecastle. Although the introduction of the Yak-36 is a big step forward it has severe limitations for a shipboard strike aircraft in that it cannot make a short take-off, only vertical. This means that the Yak-36 must have much lower endurance than the AV-8A used by the US Marines or the Sea Harrier FRS.1 used by the Royal Navy. In many minor respects the layout of the flying arrangements take second place to the 'cruiser' characteristics, particularly the shape of the forecastle, the angular shapes of the superstructure and the sheer weight and volume of armament. Nor does the second ship of the class, the *Minsk*, display any but the most minor changes, so it seems likely that the Russian designation is an accurate reflection of their hybrid nature as cruiser/carriers.

Far from being tempted to follow the line of the *Moskva* and *Kiev* Classes the US Navy remains convinced that the functions of aircraft carriers and their cruiser escorts are best kept far apart. As long as nuclear carriers continue to be built there is a need for nuclear-powered cruisers to keep pace with them and protect them, conversely using the carrier's aircraft as part of their own defences. This concept was amply proved in the late 1960s, when the carrier *Enterprise* and the *Long Beach, Bainbridge* and *Truxtun* operated together in the Vietnam War. The authorisation of a second nuclear carrier, the *Nimitz* (CVN. 68) in 1967 was therefore accompanied by approval for a nuclear cruiser, followed a year later by funds for a second ship. A third ship was planned in FY 1968 but the astronomical cost, $200 million for the first ship and $180 million for the second in 1967-68 prices, caused it to be cancelled.

The USS *California* (CGN. 36) and *South Carolina* (CGN. 37) are two of the most powerful warships in the world, and as the epitome of modern design deserve a closer look. At first glance their 9500-ton hulls seem devoid of armament, with only two single-arm launchers for the Standard SM-1 missile and two lightweight 5-inch gun mountings forward and aft. However, like other modern warships their fighting power cannot be gauged by counting gun barrels and launchers. The sensors, the surveillance and tracker radars and the massive bow-sonar, combined with a comprehensive computer suite to process their data, enable the weapons to be used far more economically and effectively than ever before. For example the SPG-60 radar can acquire air targets at a range of 75 miles and can track them automatically. As it can act as an alternative channel for missile control it provides a fifth channel to back up the four SPG-51D trackers, and its computer can handle up to 120 different targets automatically. Thus, although only five missile targets can be engaged *simultaneously*, the computer allows rapid shifts from track to track and selection of the most urgent targets. When the more advanced SM-2 missile is available the system will be even more potent, for the missile's guidance system only requires illumination by the radar in the initial and terminal phases of its flight.

Two more nuclear carriers, the *Dwight D Eisenhower* and *Carl Vinson*, followed the *Nimitz*. To provide them with escorts four more nuclear cruisers have been built, the *Virginia* Class. They are basically similar to the *California* Class, but with many minor improvements such as a helicopter hangar and an

Below: *Artist's impression of the US Navy's projected nuclear Strike Cruiser.*

improved missile launcher capable of launching both Standard surface-to-air and Asroc anti-submarine missiles.

The next step forward was a major improvement in weaponry based on a new fleet defence system called Aegis. It started life as the US Navy's Advanced Surface Missile System (ASMS) intended to provide defence against high-speed aircraft and missiles. The heart of Aegis is a new fixed-array radar with 4480 energy-radiating elements fixed into its face. A computer programmes the radar array to send out pencil-like beams and as soon as one beam picks up a target several nearby beams are directed onto it as well. This enables the Aegis SPY-1 radar to start a smooth tracking of the target within one second, when a conventional radar would still be completing its first rotation. With four SPY-1 radars, one at each corner of the superstructure, an Aegis system provides complete coverage which the SPG-62 trackers and the SM-2 missiles can exploit to the full.

In 1968-69, when development of Aegis was well advanced, the US Navy started to plan for a fleet of 30 nuclear Aegis ships. These were to have included destroyers with only one missile launcher and cruisers with two launchers, but of these only four were authorised

between 1971 and 1975 – the *Virginia* Class. Delays in the Aegis programme then resulted in the four *Virginia*'s getting the same conventional outfit of radars and missiles as the *California* Class.

Early in 1975 Congress was asked to approve a fifth *Virginia* at the same time as long-lead funds were requested for a 17,000-ton 'Strike Cruiser', or CSGN. She was to be nuclear-powered and armed with Aegis, surface-to-air missiles and Tomahawk surface-to-surface cruise missiles, but the cost was a staggering $1,500 million. Despite the vociferous claims of the nuclear lobby led by Admiral Rickover, Congress decided that the fifth *Virginia* would not be built. The strike cruiser was deferred for a year and then rejected. Repeated attempts were made to get the ship reinstated but finally in May 1977 the Senate Armed Service Committee gave its final verdict that the ship was too costly and might well have been over-designed 'for its role as a carrier escort'.

The alternative was to resurrect the Aegis-armed destroyer, based on the hull of the *Spruance* Class destroyers. On a displacement of 9000 tons these destroyers are seaworthy enough to carry out a cruiser's duties, and late in 1979 the DDG-47 Class became CG-47. However this has not stopped the authorisa-

tion of four Aegis-equipped Modified *Virginia* Class in place of the eight strike cruisers requested in 1976. To help make up the numbers of Aegis systems Congress also urged that the existing *Virginia* Class should be refitted with the system as soon as possible. However a proposal to modernise the cruiser *Long Beach* and give her Aegis was rescinded. Congress felt that her remaining 10-15 years of effective life left did not warrant the expenditure – a sad reflection of the fact that the *Long Beach* had been launched over 20 years ago.

As always the Soviet Union came up with a bigger and more impressive answer. In 1978 it was revealed that the Zhdanov yard in Leningrad is building what could be a 32,000-ton 'battle-cruiser' to be called *Kirov*. She will be nuclear-powered and armed with air-defence and long-range surface missiles, and is almost certainly intended to screen the big aircraft carrier reported under construction in the Black Sea. Also building are three new ships, a 12,000-ton expansion of the *Kara* Class. And so the cruiser-story comes full circle, with a new generation of super-cruisers about to dominate the oceans. This development, coupled with growing doubts about the cost and validity of the big strike carrier, may give the cruiser the prestige of being the most powerful warship type ever built.

Epilogue

Sadly the cruiser has not mainly proved a popular subject for ship preservers. This is because cruisers never achieved the glamour of destroyers or the majesty of battleships. There are, however, four old cruisers that have been preserved for their special associations, and happily they cover a wide spectrum of types.

The oldest of these is the protected cruiser USS *Olympia*, the last survivor of the 'New Navy' begun in the 1880s. She was launched by Union Iron Works at San Francisco in 1892 and commissioned in 1895. Her moment of glory came in April 1898 when she was the flagship of the US Navy's Asiatic Squadron under Commodore George B Dewey at the outbreak of the Spanish-American War. Dewey determined to strike an early blow at the Spanish squadron of cruisers and gunboats in the Philippines, under the command of Admiral Patricio Montojo y Pasaren, and after a hurried refit at Hong Kong he led his force across the Pacific. The resulting Battle of Manila Bay on 1 May 1898 was a one-sided affair in which the obsolescent Spanish ships were sunk with no loss to the attackers. Although the later events in Cuba had more strategic importance the *Olympia* and Dewey won their places in public affection, and so she was certainly the prime candidate for preservation.

In 1920 the ship was only one of a number of obsolete vessels destined for the scrapheap. She was reclassified as a light cruiser (CL-15) and quietly left on the Navy List until 1931. She was then reclassified as a hulk, IX-40, and retained as a naval relic. For another quarter of a century she lay in Philadelphia Navy Yard but in September 1957 responsibility for her upkeep passed to the Cruiser *Olympia* Association. She can be visited at Pier 11 North on the Delaware River, the only late nineteenth century American cruiser afloat.

A ship of similar vintage is the Russian *Aurora*, built in 1897-1903 as one of three of the *Diana* Class. Like the *Olympia* she saw action as part of the fleet sent out to the Far East during the Russo-Japanese War. However unlike most of the other Russian ships at Tsushima in 1905 she and her sister *Diana* escaped destruction and sought internment in neutral ports. During World War I she operated with the Baltic Fleet but did nothing of note until the October Revolution. The *Aurora* had been moved up the Neva River from Kronstadt to overawe the city of Leningrad, but Lenin knew that it was unlikely that her crew would open fire on the Bolsheviks if they tried to topple the Kerensky Government. The cruiser's support was essential to Lenin, and it was agreed by the small group of revolutionary sympathisers on board that if they won their comrades around to their cause the cruiser would fire a blank shell. It was the sound of this shell, heard by Lenin and his Bolsheviks, which triggered off the attack on the Winter Palace. During the assault the *Aurora* trained her searchlights on the palace. For many years people believed that she had actually shelled the defenders of the Winter Palace, but the Russians themselves put the record straight.

It is hardly surprising that the old ship occupied a special place in the Communist pantheon, she was retained long after more effective warships were scrapped, being permanently moored in the Neva from 1930. Her service to her country was not over, for during the Great Patriotic War of 1941-45 her 130mm guns were removed for use ashore in an armoured train called *Baltiyets* after carrying out bombardments of German troops in the Oranienbaum area. Left with only light AA guns she continued to help defend the city until badly damaged by enemy bombs. Fortunately she could be towed into shallow water and was raised in the summer of 1944. It was decreed by the Leningrad Soviet in August 1945 that the ship should be placed in a permanent berth in the Neva under the authority of the Nakhimov Naval Academy, as a memorial to the October Revolution.

The old ship returned up river on 17 November 1948 and can be seen today in the Nevska, a small tributary of the Neva. She is maintained as a training ship for cadets of the nearby Academy, but the small museum on board is open to the public. Although stripped of many of her original fittings she gives a clear idea of what the smaller protected cruisers of the late nineteenth century looked like. A highly detailed model of her in original condition can be seen in the Central Naval Museum.

The only armoured cruiser which survives is the Greek *Giorgios Averoff*, built in Italy in 1908-11. She had in fact been started as a speculative venture by an Italian shipyard and was launched as *Ship X* in March 1910. By February 1911 relations between Turkey and the Balkan states of Bulgaria, Montenegro, Serbia and Greece had worsened to the point of war, and in that month Greece bought the Italian cruiser. The money had been provided under the terms of the will of the Greek millionaire Giorgios Averoff, who had wished to increase his country's defences, so she was given his name.

The new cruiser was more than a match for the very elderly Turkish Navy, and her presence in the Aegean acted as a deterrent during the Balkan War without any need for her to act. She was still in commission when World War II broke out but she escaped the fate of other Greek ships in 1941 and managed to join the British at Alexandria. After a period of escorting ships in the Indian Ocean she was overhauled to allow her to accompany the forces liberating Greece in 1943. As the rest of the Royal

Hellenic Navy was in a temporary state of mutiny she had the additional honour of being the only Greek ship present when the Allies landed. When she finally paid off in 1952 she was moored off the Island of Poros, south of Athens, where she serves both as a floating museum and an adjunct of the naval academy on the island.

The Indian Navy for many years operated the old British cruiser *Achilles* as INS *Delhi*. She served with distinction from 1948, played herself in a film of the River Plate battle in 1953 and even saw active service again in 1961, when India seized Goa from Portugal. In 1973 she became a seagoing training ship, but in 1978 the time came to pay her off, 45 years after she had first commissioned at Birkenhead. There was no question of saving her as a memorial, but approval was given to preserve 'A' turret at the Defence Academy in Poona.

The latest cruiser to be preserved is the British light cruiser HMS *Belfast*. After an unsuccessful attempt to save the famous 'Shiny *Sheffield*' in the early 1960s it was realised that the HMS *Belfast* was the last wartime cruiser of the Royal Navy worth preserving. After a considerable political battle approval was given in 1971 to hand the ship over to the HMS *Belfast* Trust for mooring in a permanent berth opposite the Tower of London. She differs from the other three preserved cruisers in that she has no overriding claim to fame, apart from her role in the sinking of the battle-cruiser *Scharnhorst*. However in the absence of any preserved British battleship of the twentieth century and for want of a truly famous cruiser such as HMS *Sheffield* it was a question of *Belfast* or nothing.

Being a more modern ship, the *Belfast* gives a much more accurate impression of life on board a cruiser of World War II, from the radar plot to the triple 6-inch gun turrets and the mess-decks. Being the last of the ships designed to fight the Japanese she enshrines many of the developments inspired by the Washington Treaty, while those limitations were in force.

Apart from one or two US *Brooklyn* Class and the British 'Colony' Class in South America, these four are the only old cruisers left. It is hard to imagine any of the current cruisers having the same appeal 30 years from now, but as we have seen the cruiser tradition is a long and honourable one. There is no telling what cruisers may achieve in the future.

Above: *The* Aurora *at her mooring in the Nevska in Leningrad, 1977, by Paul Gunn.*

Guided-Missile Cruisers of the World's Navies

Country	Name	Displacement	Status
France	1 *Colbert*	8500 tons	completed 1959
	2 *Suffren* Class	5090 tons	completed 1967–70
Italy	1 *Vittorio Veneto*	7500 tons	completed 1969
	2 *Andrea Doria* Class	5000 tons	completed 1964
Netherlands	2 *Tromp* Class	4300 tons	completed 1975–76
Soviet Union	1 *Dzerzhinski*	16,000 tons	completed c1956
	4 *Kynda* Class	4400 tons	completed 1962–64
	4 *Kresta I* Class	6140 tons	completed 1967–70
	10 *Kresta II* Class	6000 tons	completed 1970–78
	10 *Kara* Class	8200 tons	completed 1973–
	3 *Kirov* Class	10,000 tons	building
	2 *Sovietsky Soyuz* Class	32,000 tons	building
Great Britain	7 *Devonshire* Class	5440 tons	completed 1963–70
	1 *Bristol*	6100 tons	completed 1973
United States	1 *Oklahoma City*★	10,570 tons	completed 1954
	2 *Albany* Class★	13,700 tons	completed 1945–46
	1 *Long Beach*	14,200 tons	completed 1961
	1 *Bainbridge*	7600 tons	completed 1962
	9 *Leahy* Class	5670 tons	completed 1962–64
	9 *Belknap* Class	6570 tons	completed 1964–67
	1 *Truxtun*	8200 tons	completed 1967
	2 *California* Class	9561 tons	completed 1974–75
	4 *Virginia* Class	8400 tons	completed 1976–80
	16 *CG-47* Class	7070 tons	building

★to be scrapped 1980–81

Index

Acknowledgements

Aldo Fraccaroli: pp9 (top), 44 (top), 75 (below), 135 (top), 138 (top), 172, 173.
British Official: pp139 (top), 160-161.
Bundesarchiv: pp13 (bottom), 14, 21 (top), 22, 29, 32-33, 35, 40-41 (bottom), 42-43 (bottom), 102 (top), 106 (top), 112 (top), 122 (top and bottom), 128 (centre), 129 (bottom), 130, 131.
C & S Taylor: p174 (bottom).
Central Naval Museum Leningrad: p20.
Claus Bergen: p81.
Conway Picture Library: pp136, 137-138.
Establissement Cinématographique et Photographique des Armées: pp75 (top), 97 (centre), 124, 166 (centre), 168-169, 171 (bottom).
Foto Drüppel: pp16 (top), 50-51, 104-105 (centre), 118-119 (bottom), 122 (centre), 126-127, 128 (top), 163 (top).
Imperial War Museum: pp10-11 (bottom), 13 (top), 15 (centre), 23 (top), 30-31, 41 (top), 42 (top), 44 (bottom), 47, 64, 120 (top), 121 (top), 100, 104-105 (bottom).
Italian Navy: pp96-97 (bottom), 97 (top), 174 (top).
Marina Militare: p80.
Marius Bar: pp178-179 (bottom).
Ministry of Defence: pp167, 170 (top and bottom), 175 (top), 176-177, 178 (top), 180, 181, 183, 184-185 (top).
Musées de la Marine: pp8-9 (bottom), 10-11 (top), 15 (top), 18, 26-27, 56-57 (top), 75 (centre), 108, 112-113 (bottom), 114-115 (bottom), 116, 166 (bottom), 184 (bottom).
National Maritime Museum: pp19 (centre and bottom), 25 (top), 48 (top), 82-83 (top), 132 (top and centre), 133, 148 (centre), 156-157, 162.
Naval Photograph Club: pp34, 103 (top), 140-141 (bottom).

Navpic: p171 (centre).
P A Vicary: pp37, 38-39 (bottom).
Preston Picture Library: pp16 (bottom), 21 (bottom), 25 (bottom), 39 (top and centre), 52, 57 (bottom), 58 (top), 111 (top), 189.
Robert Hunt Library: p17.
Roberts, John: pp92-93.
Royal Swedish Navy: pp114-115 (top), 165 (centre), 166 (bottom).
Shizuo Fukui: pp62-63, 65, 70, 71 (top), 72 (top), 73 (top), 78 (top), 98-99 (bottom), 101, 109, 141 (top), 148, 154-155.
Tass: p185 (bottom).
Slater Picture Library: pp94-95 (both).
Ullstein: pp105 (right), 106-107 (bottom), 121-122 (bottom), 129 (top), 132, 159 (bottom right).
US Air Force: p61 (bottom).
US Navy: pp6-7, 8 (top), 19 (top), 53, 54, 55, 58 (bottom), 59, 61 (top two), 68-69 (bottom), 69 (top), 71 (bottom), 72 (bottom), 73 (centre), 74-75 (bottom), 78-79, 84-85 (all three), 86-87 (both), 88-89, 90-91 (both), 92 (top), 98 (top and centre), 110-111 (bottom), 134 (bottom), 135 (bottom), 141 (bottom), 143 (top), 145 (top and bottom), 146, 147, 148 (top), 149 (bottom), 150, 151, 152, 153, 158 (top), 158-159 (bottom), 159 (top), 164 (top and bottom), 165 (top), 179 (top and centre), 182, 186-187.
Wright & Logan: pp102-103 (bottom), 119 (top), 171 (top).

The author would like to thank Richard Natkiel who drew the maps and Penny Murphy who prepared the index.